WALT DISNEY WORLD

4 TEENS BY TEENS

WALT DISNEY WORLD

4 TEENS BY TEENS

Kim Wright Wiley

Leigh Chandler Wiley

PRIMA PUBLISHING

Published by Prima Publishing, Roseville, California. Member of the Crown Publishing Group, a division of Random House, Inc.

PRIMA PUBLISHING and colophon are trademarks of Random House, Inc., registered with the United States Patent and Trademark Office.

All products mentioned in this book are trademarks of their respective companies.

Every effort has been made to make this book complete and accurate as of the date of publication. In a time of rapid change, however, it is difficult to ensure that all information is entirely up-to-date. Although the publisher and author cannot be liable for any inaccuracies or omissions in this book, they are always grateful for corrections and suggestions for improvement.

Editorial Assistant: Felicia B. Howie

Library of Congress Cataloging-in-Publication Data
Wiley, Kim Wright
    Walt Disney World 4 teens by teens : the hottest rides, coolest shows, and best places to eat and shop! / Kim Wright Wiley, Leigh Chandler Wiley.
      p. cm.
    Includes index.
    ISBN 0-7615-2627-7
    1. Walt Disney World (Fla.)—Guidebooks. 2. Family recreation—Florida—Orlando Region—Guidebooks. I.Title: Walt Disney World for teens by teens. II. Wiley, Leigh Chandler. III. Title.

GV1853.3.F62 W3486 2000
917.59'24—dc21
                                                                00-032394

02 03 04 05 BB 10 9 8 7 6 5 4 3
Printed in the United States of America

First Edition

Visit us online at www.primapublishing.com

To our friends
Brennon and Courtney Youngblood
for all their help, and to the
Good Shepherd Youth Group
for their feedback and support.

Contents

List of Maps and Quick Guides   xi
Preface   xiii

SECTION 1
WALT DISNEY WORLD   1

1 Before You Go   3

The Best Time of Year to Go   3
Map of Walt Disney World   4
Types of Tickets   7
School Projects   10
Walt Disney World Touring Tips   13
Getting Around Disney:
   Monorails, Boats, Buses, and Cars   16

2 The Magic Kingdom   21

How to Get to the Magic Kingdom   21
The Big Stuff   21
Map of the Magic Kingdom   21
Quick Guide to Magic Kingdom Attractions   24
Magic Kingdom Rides   26
Parades and Shows   35
Where to Eat   36
Where to Shop   36
Magic Kingdom "Don't Miss" List   37

3 Epcot 39

Getting to Epcot 39
Map of Epcot 40
Quick Guide to Epcot Attractions 42
The Big Stuff 44
Epcot Attractions 44
Parades and Shows 52
Where to Eat 52
Where to Shop 54
Epcot's "Don't Miss" List 54

4 The Disney-MGM Studios 55

How to Get to MGM 55
The Big Stuff 55
Map of Disney-MGM Studios 56
Quick Guide to MGM Attractions 58
MGM Attractions 60
Parades and Shows 68
Where to Eat 69
Where to Shop 69
MGM "Don't Miss" List 70

5 Animal Kingdom 71

Getting to the Animal Kingdom 71
Map of Animal Kingdom 72
Quick Guide to Animal Kingdom Attractions 74
The Big Stuff 74
Animal Kingdom Attractions 75
Where to Eat 84
Where to Shop 84
Animal Kingdom "Don't Miss" List 85

6 The Rest of the World 87

Getting to the Rest of the World 87
Map of Walt Disney World Water Parks 88
Which Water Park is Right for You? 90

Blizzard Beach   90
Typhoon Lagoon   93
River Country   95
**Map of Downtown Disney
   and Pleasure Island**   96
Downtown Disney   98
Sports at Walt Disney World   102

SECTION 2
UNIVERSAL ORLANDO   105

Map of Universal Orlando   106
Getting to Universal Orlando   109

7 Universal Studios   111

The Big Stuff   111
Universal Attractions   111
Map of Universal Studios   112
Quick Guide to Universal Attractions   114
Parades and Shows   124
Where to Eat   125
Where to Shop   125
Universal Studios "Don't Miss" List   126

8 Islands of Adventure and CityWalk   127

Map of Islands of Adventure   128
Map of CityWalk   130
Quick Guide to Islands of Adventure
   Attractions   132
The Big Stuff   134
Islands of Adventure Attractions   134
Where to Eat   143
Where to Shop   143
Islands of Adventure "Don't Miss" List   144
CityWalk   144

9 Beyond Disney World: Sea World and Other Orlando Attractions   147

Sea World   147
Discovery Cove   154
Gatorland   157
Wet 'n Wild   158
Mystery Fun House   159
Off-Site Dinner Shows
    (With or Without the Whole Fam)   159

Index   163

List of Maps and Quick Guides

Maps

Walt Disney World   4
Magic Kingdom   21
Epcot   40
Disney-MGM Studios   56
Animal Kingdom   72
Walt Disney World Water Parks   88
Downtown Disney and Pleasure Island   96
Universal Orlando   106
Universal Studios   112
Islands of Adventure   128
CityWalk   130

Quick Guides

Magic Kingdom Attractions   24
Epcot Attractions   42
MGM Attractions   58
Animal Kingdom Attractions   74
Universal Attractions   114
Islands of Adventure Attractions   132

Preface

HOW THIS BOOK CAME ABOUT

Kim says:

Ten years ago, when I first started writing my travel guide *Walt Disney World with Kids,* my daughter, Leigh, was five and my son, Jordan, was one. I was still looking for places to change diapers and hoping Peter Pan didn't scare them too badly, so the thought that I'd ever be doing a book called *Walt Disney World 4 Teens by Teens* was far, far away.

Fast forward a decade. My publishers approached me about doing a new guide directed toward teens, with Leigh as my coauthor. It took me about two seconds to convince her this was a great idea—especially when I said she could bring a few friends to Orlando to help with the research. (To give you some idea of what a tough job this is, "research" consists of riding Space Mountain three times in a row to see if it feels different in the front, middle, and back car.) Our experiences and evaluations, along with interviews with dozens of teens, both in the park and on the Internet, form the heart of this book.

Leigh says:

For most people, going to Disney World is a once-in-a-lifetime experience, but I've always felt like Disney World was really my hometown. Thanks to my mom's job, I've practically grown up there. She likes to tell the story about how I got lost in the Magic Kingdom when I was six and, although she and Dad went into hysterics, I didn't cry at all. Why should I? It was like being in my own backyard. So I was thrilled about being asked to write a book about what is truly the happiest place on earth. For me, anyway.

Probably one of the biggest complaints I've heard about Disney World is that it's strictly for kids, with nothing interesting for teenagers. Well, contrary to this belief, in the past three years Disney World has added new attractions specifically aimed for teens—Rock 'n' Roller Coaster at MGM, Test Track in Epcot, Countdown to Extinction and Kali River Rapids in the Animal Kingdom, and Disney Quest at Downtown Disney. But even among the older rides, there's more variety than most people realize. What's great about Disney is that they don't have one park for teens, one park for kids, and another park for adults. At every park, there are attractions for guests of all ages. (Disney always calls the tourists who visit the parks "guests," and the park employees "cast members.")

Last December I went down to Orlando with my little brother, Jordan, and two of my friends, Brennon and Courtney Youngblood. They teased me like crazy, but I made us go to the Magic Kingdom and ride It's a Small World first. That was my favorite ride as a child, and it was all about symbolism, but I guess the symbolism was too heavy for them. Another thing—ever since I was a kid, I've wanted to work for Disney as an imagineer, one of the people who design the rides, restaurants, and hotels. I've always loved the fact that all the Disney employees are so nice. So, in order to get ready for my ultimate career—even when I feel like killing someone—I've tried to act nice. And it works . . . most of the time.

Walt Disney World

Before You Go

THE BEST TIME OF YEAR TO GO

Walt Disney World is open 365 days a year, so you *can* go anytime, but during some months of the year the crowds and the weather are better than others. Disney World basically has two seasons.

"On-season" is summer and major holidays, such as Thanksgiving, Christmas, New Year's, Easter, and spring break. The good thing about going during the on-season is that the parks are open long hours—sometimes until midnight—and major shows run every day. And you don't have to miss school. The bad part about going during the on-season? It's crowded—repeat, *crowded*—and you may have to wait as long as two hours for major rides. And you don't have to miss school.

Helpful Hint

To check the theme park hours of operation for the days you'll be visiting, call 407-824-4321.

3

1. Coronado Springs Resort
2. Wide World of Sports
3. Swan Resort
4. Dolphin Resort
5. Yacht & Beach Club Resorts
6. Disney's BoardWalk
7. Magic Kingdom Main Entrance
8. Car Care Center
9. Transportation & Ticket Center Parking
10. Transportation & Ticket Center
11. Polynesian Resort
12. The Grand Floridian
13. Contemporary Resort
14. Wilderness Lodge
15. Fort Wilderness Campground
16. Dixie Landings Resort
17. Port Orleans Resort
18. Old Key West Resort
19. Lake Buena Vista Golf Course
20. Disney Institute
21. Disney Institute Villas
22. Disney's West Side
23. Pleasure Island
24. Caribbean Beach Resort
25. Animal Kingdom
26. Disney Village Hotels
27. All-Star Resorts

Magic Kingdom

Floridian Way

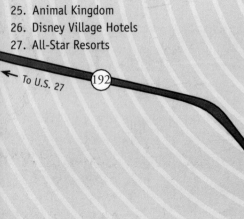

← To U.S. 27   192

Animal Kingdom

Buena Vista Dr.

Helpful Hint

For information about park hours, and anything else, for the week you'll be going, log on to www.disneyworld.com.

"Off-season" times are those fall, winter, and spring weeks that aren't near holidays. There are fewer people in the parks and the lines are way shorter. If you want to ride Rock 'n' Roller Coaster ten times in a row, it's no problem. Disadvantages? The parks don't run those mega-hours, and they may close as early as 6 or 7 P.M. Major shows like the evening parade in the Magic Kingdom and Fantasmic! at MGM only run a couple of nights a week, so you have to plan ahead to make sure you're in the right park on the right night. And in January, sometimes the water parks are closed for repairs.

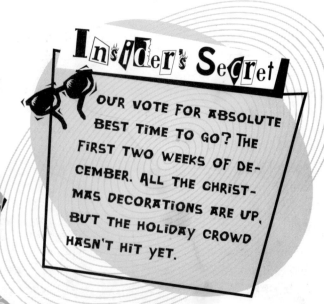

Insider's Secret

OUR VOTE FOR ABSOLUTE BEST TIME TO GO? THE FIRST TWO WEEKS OF DECEMBER. ALL THE CHRISTMAS DECORATIONS ARE UP, BUT THE HOLIDAY CROWD HASN'T HIT YET.

Types of Tickets

Disney World has more types of tickets than Snow White has dwarfs. If you're going with a school or church group, you'll be issued special group-rate tickets, and this section won't apply to you. Otherwise, you need to decide how many days you want to be in the theme parks and if you want to visit the water parks. All Park Hopper passes get you into the four major parks—that is, the Magic Kingdom, Epcot, Disney-MGM Studios, and the Animal Kingdom. The Park Hopper Plus passes get you into the water parks as well.

As we went to press, the following ticket prices (not including tax) were accurate, but Disney "adjusts"— that is, raises—prices on a regular basis, and sometimes they release new kinds of tickets as well. To make sure the prices haven't changed, call 407-824-4321.

Insider's Secret

GET THE PARK HOPPER OPTION IF YOU CAN, SO YOU CAN VISIT MORE THAN ONE PARK IN A DAY.

Seven-Day Park Hopper Plus
With this pass, you get into the four major parks, plus four visits to the minor ones.
Adult: $296
Child (three to nine): $242

Six-Day Park Hopper Plus
You get into the four major parks, plus three visits to the minor ones.
Adult: $266
Child (three to nine): $217

Five-Day Park Hopper Plus
You get into the four major parks, plus two visits to the minor ones.
Adult: $236
Child (three to nine): $192

Five-Day Park Hopper Pass
You get into the four major parks.
Adult: $206
Child (three to nine): $167

Four-Day Park Hopper Pass
You get into the four major parks.
Adult: $176
Child (three to nine): $142

One-Day Ticket
You can go to one park only.
Adult: $46
Child (three to nine): $37

Helpful Hint

If you're staying at an on-site Disney hotel, you have another ticket option—a Length of Stay Pass, which is good for four to ten days and includes access to all the major and minor parks. Obviously, the cost is tied to how long you'll be staying, but the price is a little cheaper than buying tickets at the gate.

Insider's Secret

IN THE OFF-SEASON, WHEN THE MAGIC KINGDOM CLOSES EARLY, DISNEY SOMETIMES OFFERS A SPECIAL E-TICKET (COST: $10) TO ON-SITE HOTEL GUESTS TO BE USED ALONG WITH THEIR MULTIDAY PASS. THE E-TICKET ALLOWS YOU INTO THE MAGIC KINGDOM ON A NIGHT

WHEN IT IS CLOSED TO THE GENERAL PUBLIC, AND ABOUT TEN ATTRACTIONS, INCLUDING BIG-NAME RIDES LIKE SPACE MOUNTAIN AND SPLASH MOUNTAIN, ARE OPEN. SINCE ONLY ABOUT FIVE THOUSAND E-TICKETS ARE SOLD A NIGHT, THE LINES ARE VERY SHORT. IF YOU WANT TO RIDE THE COASTERS OVER AND OVER WITH NO WAITING, HERE'S YOUR CHANCE.

SCHOOL PROJECTS

Hey, we think the best time to visit Disney is during the school year when it's not so crowded. Mrs. Oster-waltz back in Geometry II might not agree. If you'll be missing school for the trip, here are some ways to make it easier.

First off, tell your teachers and coaches up front about the trip, instead of springing it on them the day before you leave. Some weeks are easier to miss than others. If you're gone during exam week or when the school has planned standardized testing, or you're missing a major game, your teacher or coach won't be happy. Also, do as much of your make-up work as you can in advance. The post-trip crash is bad enough without facing three hours of make-up work each night of the first week you're back.

You can also offer to do a special project based on your trip. Here are some suggestions:

✿ *At Epcot, the greenhouse tour in the Land pavilion is full of information on space-age farming, and marine biology is the theme of the Living Seas pavilion.*

✿ *Do a plant study of the Cretaceous Trail in the Animal Kingdom, which traces the botanical evolution of plants that have survived from the Cretaceous period.*

✿ *The Conservation Station in the Animal Kingdom is the park's research hub, where students can tour veterinary labs, use the Eco-Web to get information on conservation organizations, and watch interactive videos about endangered animals.*

✿ *Missing Geography class? Or foreign language? Head over to Epcot's World Showcase, where you* can experience the architecture, history, music, and food of eleven countries. The pavilions are staffed by college-age students from the nation represented, so you can try out your French or German on a native speaker. (Don't worry—they're trained not to laugh when you say things like "I am a pencil" in Italian, and they all speak perfect English in case your Spanish falls apart.) The cast members are always eager to talk to park guests—especially if you look for someone who is working a shop or drink stand that doesn't happen to be crowded at the moment—so you can even do a short interview about how life in the United States is different from the way teenagers live in their home country.

❁ Missing English class? Offer either to keep a journal of your trip or to interview someone about what it's like to work for Disney.

❁ Math is a bit trickier, but it should be easy to come up with a series of math-based problems, such as: If 49,000 people visit Walt Disney World on a typical day in March, and a third of them are children, and one-day tickets are $46 for adults, and $37 for kids, how much money does Disney take in that day on admissions alone? Or figure how many miles a day a Test Track car covers, or how many pounds of human flesh go down Runoff Rapids at Blizzard Beach in a typical hour.

The Disney Institute

Try a class at the Disney Institute. Don't worry—the classes here are lots more fun than those at home. For starters, as you can see below, you won't even be in a classroom. Either call the Disney Institute (800-746-5858) for an information packet or visit their Web site at www.disneyinstitute.com. A half-day class is usually $69, but some classes have additional fees, so be sure to check. The following programs are for students age eleven to fifteen:

✿ *Animation Magic (3.5 hours): You learn the tricks of the trade from Disney artists by going backstage at the animation studio, painting a cel, and getting tips on drawing the characters.*

✿ *The Magic Behind the Show (3.5 hours): You go behind the scenes at the Magic Kingdom to see how a live show is prepared, as well as look at the technical side of the production. You visit the famous Magic Kingdom "tunnel" to see the world's largest costume department and meet cast members who talk about show business, Disney-style.*

FunFactoid

Ever noticed that you never see a cast member walking through Fantasyland in a Frontierland costume? Legend has it that the Magic Kingdom is built over a series of complex tunnels through which merchandise is delivered, trash is removed, and cast members come and go to their jobs. Well, the "utiladoor" system really does exist, but it isn't a tunnel. All the behind-the-scenes work is done on the ground level; the whole Magic Kingdom is really on the second floor.

❀ *Disney Made Wild (3.5 hours): Discover how nature inspires the magic of Disney parks, especially the Animal Kingdom, where the plants were grown from scratch using seeds and cuttings Disney imagineers have collected from all around the world.*

Sixteen or over? You can take adult classes at the Disney Institute, which include cooking, photography, rock climbing, and animation. Actual offerings vary from week to week, so call 800-746-5858 or check the Web site at www.disneyinstitute.com to see what's available while you're in Orlando. Or you might enjoy the behind-the-scenes tours: One takes you through the Magic Kingdom tunnel system and another gives you the ultimate insider scoop on Epcot's World Showcase. Call 407-WDW-TOUR for details.

WALT DISNEY WORLD TOURING TIPS

Before you get to the park, make sure you pick up a few crucial items. Don't leave home without:

❀ *Comfortable shoes. Some people wear slides or sandals to the park. Bad, bad, bad, bad idea.*

❀ *A bathing suit. It's usually warm enough to swim in Florida all year.*

❀ *A lightweight, waterproof jacket. Or, if it starts raining while you're there, Disney sells bright yellow plastic ponchos for $5 all over the parks.*

❀ *Sunglasses and/or wide-brimmed hats to shade your face.*

❀ *Sunscreen. You need it year-round in Florida, not just in summer.*

❀ *A phone calling card. Hotels have surcharges of up to 40 percent on long-distance calls, so use a card and a pay phone when you can.*

✿ *Extra film. You can get it in the parks, but at primo prices.*

✿ *A beach towel. The rental towels at the water parks are pitiful.*

✿ *A waist pouch or fanny pack to keep your hands free while loading onto rides. If you have something heavy to tote, like a camcorder, bring a backpack.*

✿ *A waterbottle. Drinks are expensive in the parks—try $2.50 for bottled water and $3 for a Coke. Bring your own water bottle and refill it when you can.*

✿ *A waterproof, disposable camera. A must-have if you're visiting the water parks.*

Then, once you get to the park, keep the following tips in mind to maximize your visit.

✿ *Get there early. This isn't a vacation for planning and resting—you gotta move! And if you're staying at a Disney hotel, they have something called early entry mornings where you can get into one park a day an hour ahead of the rest of the people. This is a good chance to ride the popular rides before the crowds get too bad.*

✿ *Once you get to the parks, ride the main attractions first.*

✿ *Each park has a tip board that lists the approximate wait times for rides. It's there for a reason, so check it out. You might find a sixty-minute wait at Tower of Terror but just a ten-minute wait at Star Tours.*

✿ *Park Hop. Spend your morning in one park and your afternoon in another.*

✿ *Use the FASTPASS to cut down on the time you spend in line. Here's how it works: You enter the gate and head toward a popular ride, where a digital clock shows you the approximate wait time and the return time for a FASTPASS. This is usually a one-hour time slot. For instance, let's say the line at Test Track is way too long and the FASTPASS return time is 12:30 to 1:30 P.M. Insert your theme park ticket into the FASTPASS machine, get your ticket back along with the FASTPASS, and then go do whatever you want. Come back between 12:30 and 1:30, and you'll go through a separate turnstile just for FASTPASS people and have a much shorter wait. Short like ten minutes instead of ninety. It's a great system, but there's one catch: You can only get one FASTPASS at a time.*

Insider's Secret

DURING SUMMERS AND HOLIDAYS, FASTPASS IS ALSO AVAILABLE AT: WINNIE THE POOH, JUNGLE CRUISE, AND BUZZ LIGHTYEAR IN THE MAGIC KINGDOM; HONEY, I SHRUNK THE AUDIENCE IN EPCOT; AND INDIANA JONES AND LITTLE MERMAID AT MGM.

❀ *Rides that offer a FASTPASS are Splash Mountain and Space Mountain at the Magic Kingdom; Countdown to Extinction, Kali River Rapids, and Kilimanjaro Safaris at the Animal Kingdom; Test Track at Epcot; and Tower of Terror and Rock 'n' Roller Coaster at MGM.*

GETTiNG AROUND DiSNEY: MONORAiLS, BOATS, BUSES, AND CARS

Monorails

There are three basic monorail routes at Walt Disney World. Route one runs between the Ticket and Transportation Center (a sort of train station near the Magic Kingdom) and Epcot. The second route (the "express") makes a continuous circle between the Ticket and Transportation Center (TTC) and the Magic Kingdom. The third route (the "local") makes another continuous circle, this one between the TTC and the Magic Kingdom, but in addition it stops at the three Disney hotels, the Polynesian, the Contemporary, and the Grand Floridian.

The monorails are fast and hold a lot of people, so they're usually your quickest means of getting around. You'll basically take a monorail in one of three situations:

Q&A

Q: How long do the drivers train to run the monorail?

A: A week. Considering how long you spent in driver's ed., does that seem fair?

Insider's Secret

WHILE WAITING FOR THE MONORAIL, ASK THE ATTENDANT IF THE DRIVER'S CAB IS VACANT. THERE'S ROOM FOR UP TO FIVE PEOPLE TO RIDE IN FRONT WITH THE DRIVER. HE OR SHE WILL TELL YOU ALL ABOUT THE MONORAIL, AND THE FRONT CAB GIVES YOU GREAT VIEWS, ESPECIALLY IF YOU'RE GOING FROM THE MAGIC KINGDOM TO EPCOT.

✿ *If you arrive at the Magic Kingdom by car, you park in the parking lot and take a tram to the TTC. From there, you can board an express monorail to either the Magic Kingdom or Epcot.*

✿ *If you want to go between the Magic Kingdom and Epcot, you must take the express monorail to the TTC and transfer to the other park's monorail. It's the same process going in either direction.*

✿ *If you're a guest at the Polynesian, the Grand Floridian, or the Contemporary, lucky you—hop on the monorail and you'll be at the Magic Kingdom in minutes.*

Boats

Disney World has a huge waterway system and a whole fleet of boats to get guests around. You'll be riding one on these occasions.

✿ *From the TTC, a ferryboat (as well as the mono-rail) can take you to the Magic Kingdom.*

✿ *Guests at Wilderness Lodge, Fort Wilderness, the Polynesian, the Grand Floridian, and the Contemporary all have boat service to the Magic Kingdom.*

✿ *Another waterway connects Epcot and MGM. To find the water taxi at Epcot, leave through the backdoor exit between France and the United Kingdom in the World Showcase. Either walk or take the shuttle taxi to the Yacht and Beach Club dock, and then transfer to the MGM water taxi. At MGM, the water taxi is docked to the left as you exit.*

✿ *Guests at the Yacht and Beach Club, the Board-Walk, the Swan, and the Dolphin resorts have direct water taxi service to both Epcot and MGM.*

✿ *Another waterway connects Downtown Disney to the following Disney resorts: Port Orleans, Dixie Landings, and Disney's Old Key West. You can also use the boats to go from Downtown Disney Marketplace to Downtown Disney West Side.*

Buses

Buses are the most common way of getting around Disney World for the people staying on Disney property. They connect all the Disney resorts to the major and minor parks.

If you're staying off-site, your non-Disney hotel may also run shuttle buses to the major parks, though very few run buses to the minor parks.

Cars

Orlando is a pretty easy town to drive in, since it's prepared for lots of tourists and everything is well marked. If you happen to miss an exit once you're on the grounds of Walt Disney World, don't try to turn off the road and go back. The roads are basically big circles, so you'll get another chance at an exit within a mile or two.

All the major and minor parks have parking lots. There's a $6 parking fee at the major parks, and no charge at the minor. At the Animal Kingdom, MGM, and Epcot, you just park and take the shuttle to the entrance gate. At the Magic Kingdom, you take a shuttle from the parking lot to the TTC, and from there either take the monorail or the ferryboat to the Magic Kingdom or take the monorail to Epcot.

Helpful Hint

Definitely, definitely, definitely write down the number of the row where you park. Pluto 43 might be easy to remember now, but your brain may not be able to retrieve this information after fourteen straight hours on Space Mountain!!!

Sounds confusing, huh? Well, the Disney transportation system can be overwhelming at first, although you'll soon get it down. People staying at the Disney hotels get a transportation guide when they check in. It has a handy chart telling them exactly how to get from Port Orleans to the Wide World of Sports or from MGM to Downtown Disney—or to and from any of the hundreds of possible destinations in this huge, spread-out complex known as Walt Disney

World. If you're staying off-site and have a Park Hopper ticket, you can use Disney transportation, too; just ask for a transportation guide in the Guest Relations office at any of the parks. Or ask a cast member for help.

2

The Magic Kingdom

The Magic Kingdom is not just for little kids. We'll admit it's probably the park most oriented toward kids, but it's also the park with the most fame. When people think Disney, they usually think Cinderella's Castle, Dumbo, Space Mountain—all of which are in the Magic Kingdom.

HOW TO GET TO THE MAGIC KINGDOM

If you're staying at a Disney hotel: From the Contemporary, Grand Floridian, or Polynesian, take the monorail. From Wilderness Lodge, take the boat. From any other hotel, take the bus, which will deliver you right to the Magic Kingdom gates.

If you're not staying at a Disney hotel: Take your hotel shuttle or your car to the Magic Kingdom parking lot. Catch the shuttle to the Ticket and Transportation Center (TTC). From there take either the monorail or the ferryboat to the Magic Kingdom gates.

THE BIG STUFF

We surveyed over a hundred teens and their advice was head toward the three mountains—Space, Splash, and Big Thunder. Try to ride these early in the morning before the lines get too long.

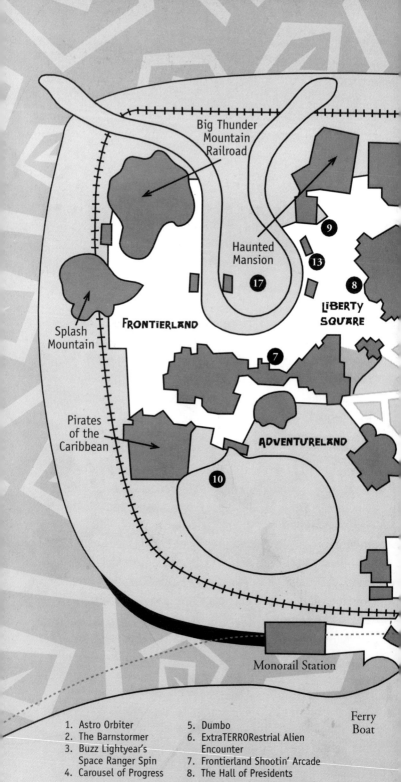

Big Thunder
Mountain
Railroad

Haunted
Mansion

⑨

⑬

⑧

⑰

LIBERTY
SQUARE

FRONTIERLAND

Splash
Mountain

⑦

Pirates
of the
Caribbean

ADVENTURELAND

⑩

Monorail Station

Ferry
Boat

1. Astro Orbiter
2. The Barnstormer
3. Buzz Lightyear's
   Space Ranger Spin
4. Carousel of Progress

5. Dumbo
6. ExtraTERRORestrial Alien
   Encounter
7. Frontierland Shootin' Arcade
8. The Hall of Presidents

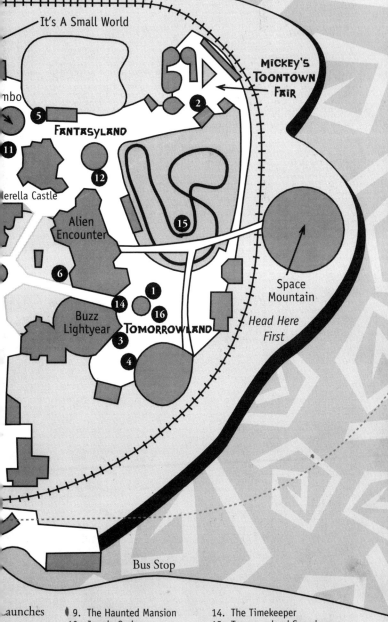

Magic Kingdom

It's A Small World

Mickey's
Toontown
Fair

2

5

FANTASYLAND

11

12

erella Castle

Alien
Encounter

Space
Mountain

*Head Here
First*

6

1

14

16

Buzz
Lightyear

3

TOMORROWLAND

4

Bus Stop

aunches   9. The Haunted Mansion   14. The Timekeeper
10. Jungle Cruise   15. Tomorrowland Speedway
11. Legend of the Lion King   16. Tomorrowland Transit
12. Mad Tea Party   Authority
13. Mike Fink Keelboats   17. Tom Sawyer Island

Quick Guide to

Attraction	Location
Astro Orbiter	Tomorrowland
Big Thunder Mountain Railroad	Frontierland
Buzz Lightyear's Space Ranger Spin	Tomorrowland
Carousel of Progress	Tomorrowland
Cinderella's Golden Carrousel	Fantasyland
Country Bear Jamboree	Frontierland
Diamond Horseshoe Jamboree	Frontierland
Dumbo	Fantasyland
The Enchanted Tiki Birds	Adventureland
ExtraTERRORestrial Alien Encounter	Tomorrowland
Goofy's Barnstormer	Toontown
The Hall of Presidents	Liberty Square
The Haunted Mansion	Liberty Square
It's a Small World	Fantasyland
Jungle Cruise	Adventureland
Legend of the Lion King	Fantasyland
Liberty Square Riverboat	Liberty Square
Mad Tea Party	Fantasyland
The Many Adventures of Winnie the Pooh	Fantasyland
Mike Fink Keelboats	Liberty Square
Peter Pan's Flight	Fantasyland

Magic Kingdom Attractions

Speed of Line	Duration of Ride/Show	Scare Factor	Cool Factor
Slow	2 min.	!!	✔✔
Moderate	3 min.	!!	✔✔✔
Fast	6 min.	!	✔✔✔
Fast	22 min.	!	✔
Slow	2 min.	!	✔
Moderate	15 min.	!	✔
Fast	30 min.	!	✔
Slow	1.5 min.	!	✔
Fast	20 min.	!	✔
Fast	20 min.	!!!	✔✔✔
Fast	20 min.	!	✔✔
Slow	1 min.	!	✔
Slow	9 min.	!!	✔✔
Fast	11 min.	!	✔
Slow	10 min.	!	✔
Moderate	25 min.	!	✔
Fast	15 min.	!	✔
Slow	2 min.	!!	✔✔
Moderate	5 min.	!	✔
Slow	15 min.	!	✔
Moderate	3 min.	!	✔

(continues)

Quick Guide to

Attraction	Location
Pirates of the Caribbean	Adventureland
Snow White's Scary Adventures	Fantasyland
Space Mountain	Tomorrowland
Splash Mountain	Frontierland
Swiss Family Robinson Treehouse*	Adventureland
The Timekeeper	Tomorrowland
Tomorrowland Speedway	Tomorrowland
Tomorrowland Transit Authority	Tomorrowland
Tom Sawyer Island	Frontierland

Scare Factor
  ! = Even your grandmother could ride this!
 !! = A couple of **GOTCHA**! moments.
!!! = Serious thrills here!

*According to WDW, this ride will soon be redesigned to become Tarzan's Treehous

MAGIC KINGDOM RIDES

Tomorrowland

Space Mountain: This coaster is like po-
tato chips; once you start, it's hard
to stop. Space Mountain
only goes 28 mph, but
since the ride takes place
in total darkness, it feels
like you're going a whole
lot faster.

"Space Mountain is best
coaster in the park!"
Mica, 14

Magic Kingdom Attractions

Speed of Line	Duration of Ride/Show	Scare Factor	Cool Factor
Fast	8 min.	!!	✔✔
Slow	2.5 min.	!	✔
Moderate	3 min.	!!!	✔✔✔
Moderate	10 min.	!!	✔✔✔
Slow	20 min.	!	✔
Fast	20 min.	!	✔
Slow	5 min.	!	✔
Fast	10 min.	!	✔
Slow	n/a	!	✔

Cool Factor

✔ = Totally lame!
✔✔ = Might be fine if you have time.
✔✔✔ = Don't miss this ride!

Insider's Secret

HANG ONTO YOUR STUFF. CAST MEMBERS TOLD US THEY FIND ALL SORTS OF STUFF AT THE BOTTOM OF SPACE MOUNTAIN.

Insider's Secret

RIDE ONCE, THEN GET A FASTPASS. COME BACK ABOUT 15 MINUTES BEFORE THE FASTPASS ACTIVATES, SINCE ON SPACE MOUNTAIN EVEN THE FASTPASS LINE CAN GET CROWDED.

Buzz Lightyear's Space Ranger Spin: This is designed to be a huge video game, in which you ride through in cars with guns and shoot at targets. Hit the bull's-eyes to score points, and at the end of the ride, you'll find out if you're a Space Ace or a puny trainee. Can you spell A-D-D-I-C-T-I-V-E?

Insider's Secret

AT BUZZ LIGHTYEAR, YOU GET MORE POINTS FOR HITTING TARGETS THAT ARE FAR AWAY OR MOVING. BUT IF YOU'RE A LOUSY SHOT, JUST AIM FOR SOMETHING CLOSE AND HIT IT A LOT.

"*Buzz Lightyear* is a great cool down after Space Mountain, especially if it freaked you out."

Jamie, 16

Scare Factor

Want to really spin? Ride alone and you'll control the car better!

ExtraTERRORestrial Alien Encounter: The alien gets loose. And wants to eat *you*. Or something to that effect. People are screaming so loud, it's hard to hear the story, but the bottom line is that this giant lobster-thing gets so close you feel its breath on your neck and its scales slithering around you. Oh yeah, did we mention it takes place in the dark?

"The special effects at *Alien Encounter* are awesome, especially because you feel more things than you see."

Cassie, 15

Timekeeper: Split opinions on this show: some teens think it's funny, some say it's stupid. Robin Williams plays the Timekeeper who takes you back in time, and the show takes place in a circular theater with a 360-degree screen. You have to stand up for the whole thing, so don't go if you're tired, and don't get stuck behind some tall guy in a Goofy hat.

Astro Orbiter: This is Dumbo for adults, except you go around in rockets, not elephants. Fun at night, when Tomorrowland is all lit up below, but definitely not a good choice just after you've eaten.

The rest of Tomorrowland: Tomorrowland's Indy Speedway is strictly for kids, who'll get off on driving pokey little race cars around a track. Carousel of Progress is a good place to park the 'rents while you're doing Space Mountain. Tomorrowland Transit Authority is just a little tram that goes in circles.

"Tomorrowland Transit Authority is a good place to make out because you go through **Space Mountain** and it's totally dark in there."

Kelly, 15

Adventureland
Pirates of the Caribbean: If you like those audio-animatronic robot people, you'll love Pirates of the Caribbean. Plus it's got a great song. You take a boat ride back to when pirates grabbed whatever they could. And all the drunken pirates look real, right down to the hair on their legs.

Jungle Cruise: Walt Disney originally wanted this ride to have real animals, but when he found

Insider's Secret

IF YOU HAVEN'T BEEN ON PIRATES OF THE CARIBBEAN FOR A COUPLE OF YEARS, YOU MAY NOTICE SOME CHANGES. THE PIRATES ARE NOW POLITICALLY CORRECT: INSTEAD OF CHASING THE WOMEN, THE WOMEN CHASE THEM.

out they would mostly sleep through the day, he went with really fake-looking audio-animatronics. Who wants to see a plastic rhino when you can check out the real thing at the Animal Kingdom?

Swiss Family Robinson Treehouse: Semi-neat re-creation of the treehouse from the movie. The plumbing system is the best part. It takes eight hundred steps to get up and down, so think of this as your workout for the day.

Enchanted Tiki Birds: Iago from *Aladdin* and Zazu from the *Lion King* have teamed up to buy the Tiki Bird Show and give it a new kick. As usual, Iago gives it the wrong kick and ticks off the Tiki gods. A pretty funny show if you're tired and right outside at the Dole stand, where you can buy some killer pineapple drinks.

Frontierland

Splash Mountain: It's a kiddie theme, but the story of Brer Rabbit being chased by Brer Fox is cute, and you've got that Zip-a-Dee-Doo-Dah theme song, too. There are several teaser drops before the big one at the end. Be sure to raise your arms, so you'll look good for the picture.

Insider's Secret

WANT TO GET WET WITHOUT GOING ON SPLASH MOUNTAIN? STAND ON THE BRIDGE IN FRONT OF THE RIDE—EVERY THIRD OR FOURTH LOG THAT DROPS SETS OFF A MAJOR SPLASH.

"To get really soaked at Splash Mountain, sit in the front seat."

Alex, 13

Big Thunder Mountain Railroad: This coaster is a runaway train that takes you through an old mining village. The ride is major fun, and there's lots to look at. It's more of a rattle-you-around ride than a big drop coaster, so even people with a fear of heights can ride.

> "Thunder Mountain is my favorite ride in the whole world."
>
> Leigh, 15

Other Frontierland Attractions: Tom Sawyer's Island is strictly for kids, and so is the Country Bear Jamboree, which is so cute it will make you gag. The Diamond Horseshoe Jamboree is funny if one of your friends gets dragged into the show with the saloon girls, but definitely not funny if you're the one they pick.

Liberty Square

Haunted Mansion: Everybody loves this ride, with its stretching rooms and 999 Happy Haunts (but

Insider's Secret

THERE ARE HIDDEN MICKEYS ALL OVER WALT DISNEY WORLD—MICKEY MOUSE SHAPES YOU CAN SEE IN CARPETS, PAINTED CLOUDS, AND EVEN SEWER COVERS. BUT THE HAUNTED MANSION HAS THE ONLY HIDDEN DONALD. LOOK CLOSELY AT THE CHAIR ON YOUR RIGHT JUST AFTER YOU PASS THE CORPSE THAT'S TRYING TO ESCAPE FROM HIS COFFIN.

there's always room for one more). You ride through in these black "doom buggies," and the cast members who load you in are dressed like morticians and never smile. Check out the gravestones while you wait in line . . . the names on the tombs are the imagineers who worked on the ride. And when you leave, look for the pet cemetery on your left.

The House of Presidents: After a long boring film on U.S. history, the curtain rises to reveal an audio-animatronic figure of every president from George Washington to Bill Clinton. The thrill lasts about two seconds—but the show lasts about thirty minutes. Then Clinton makes a speech: "No, I did not have sexual relations . . ." Just kidding. A must-skip, unless you're *really* into history.

Other Liberty Square rides: The riverboat goes in a big circle around Tom Sawyer's Island. Yawn. The keelboats also go in a big circle around Tom Sawyer's Island, and the pilots torture you with silly jokes.

Fantasyland and Mickey's Toontown

It's a Small World: You know the song, but have you seen the ride? It's incredibly cute, with all these dolls representing children from around the world.

Peter Pan: You fly in pirate ships above scenes from the movie. The ride actually tells a story . . . which is more than we can say for some of the others in Fantasyland. Look for Tinkerbell as you lift off.

"My favorite part of **Peter Pan** is when you pass Hook and he's being eaten by a crocodile, and Smee can't help him."

Courtney, 13

Dumbo: A totally classic ride, the one you see in all the ads. You can make it jerky and cool if you yank the joystick. But the line gets really long, so ride it late at night after all the kiddies have gone home.

Winnie the Pooh: You ride through in honey pots, and the ride is kind of neat if you like Winnie the Pooh (and Tigger, too.) Sniff out Pooh's Thotful Shop as you exit—it smells like honey.

The Mad Tea Party: The tea cups are definitely the best teen attraction in Fantasyland. You totally control the speed.

In**s**i**d**er**'**s Se**c**r**e**t

AT THE MAD TEA PARTY,
DON'T LET MORE THAN TWO
PEOPLE SPIN YOUR TEA CUP.
IT CAN GET COMPLICATED TO
SYNCHRONIZE YOUR MOVES,
AND YOU JUST END UP
GOING SLOWER.

Goofy's Barnstormer: The only ride in Toontown, this coaster lasts for a whole fifty-eight seconds, so only try it if the line is short. It's wilder than it looks, maybe because you-know-who is the pilot.

Meeting Mickey: Feeling retro? Go to Toontown, line up in Mickey's house, and get your picture taken with the main mouse.

Other Fantasyland attractions: Snow White's Scary Adventures aren't, and the carousel is just like a zillion others. If you're a fan of the movie, you might want to check out the Lion King show.

PARADES AND SHOWS

The Magic Kingdom has two major parades, the 3 P.M. one and the electric parade at night. The night parade is by far the coolest, but don't bother videotaping it because Ashley and Meg at home don't want to see it. Trust me. They don't. They have incredible fireworks after the parade, and just before they start, look up at the highest window in Cinderella's Castle and you'll see Tinkerbell's Flight. A girl dressed like Tink slides on a wire from the top of the castle to the ground.

WHERE TO EAT

Food in the Magic Kingdom is pretty lame. Cinderella's Castle is the prettiest place to eat, or if you like Italian, try Tony's Town Square Café. (You'll need to make reservations in advance; call from your room if you're staying at a Disney hotel, or make them first thing in the morning at the restaurant if you're not.)

For the fastest fast food, head to Cosmic Ray's Starlight Café in Tomorrowland. For tame Tex-Mex, try the Mile Long Bar in Frontierland. Need sugar? They have great sundaes at the Sealtest Ice Cream Parlor on Main Street and yummy chocolate chip cookies at the Main Street bakery. In fact, we say snack the whole time at the Magic Kingdom and save your food bucks for MGM or Epcot, where the restaurants are a thousand times better.

WHERE TO SHOP

The Main Street Emporium and Disney Clothiers have a bit of everything, including some good sorta-cheap stuff to bring home to friends. If you're in the market for a watch, they have the best selection at Uptown Jewelers.

MAGIC KINGDOM "DON'T MISS" LIST

- *Space Mountain*
- *Alien Encounter*
- *Buzz Lightyear*
- *Big Thunder Mountain*
- *Splash Mountain*

Rest

3

Epcot

←——————————————————→

Most people think that Epcot is total education—Disney's way of saying, "We're going to hold you down and teach you whether you like it or not," and where you have to watch a film with some dork who couldn't tell a joke to save his life. Well, wrong. Even though the majority of Epcot is made up of shows that teach you something like, "Stretch your imagination," or "Conserve energy, it's important," Disney has done a great job of bringing in humor and high-tech special effects.

Epcot consists of two sections: Future World (think science) and the World Showcase (think geography).

GETTING TO EPCOT

If you're staying at the Contemporary, Polynesian, or Grand Floridian, take the monorail to the TTC and transfer to the Epcot monorail. If you're staying at the Yacht and Beach Club, Boardwalk, Swan, or Dolphin, either take the water taxi or walk to Epcot's "back door" entrance through the World Showcase. Guests of other Disney hotels can catch a bus.

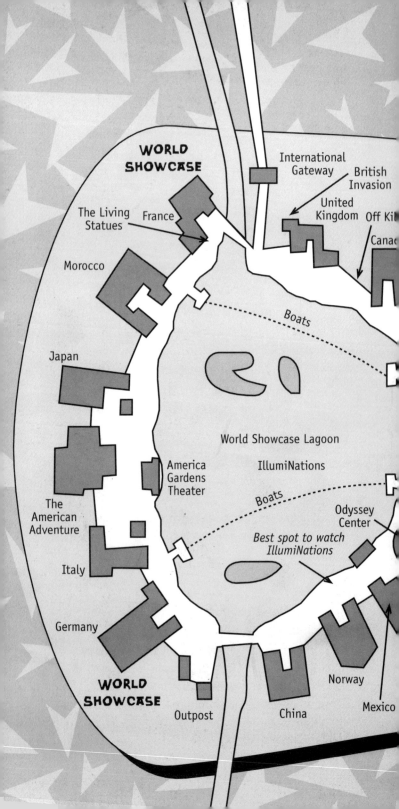

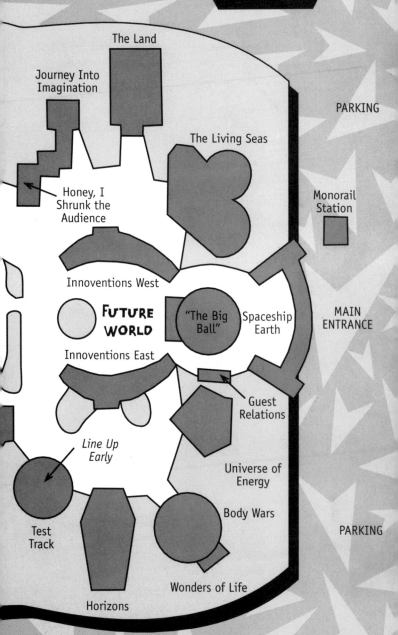

EPCOT

The Land

Journey Into Imagination

PARKING

The Living Seas

Honey, I Shrunk the Audience

Monorail Station

Innoventions West

FUTURE WORLD

"The Big Ball"

Spaceship Earth

MAIN ENTRANCE

Innoventions East

Guest Relations

Line Up Early

Universe of Energy

Body Wars

Test Track

Wonders of Life

PARKING

Horizons

Quick Guide to

Attraction	Location
Body Wars	Future World
Circle of Life	Future World
Cranium Command	Future World
Food Rocks	Future World
Honey, I Shrunk the Audience	Future World
Image Works	Future World
Innoventions	Future World
Journey into Imagination	Future World
The Living Seas	Future World
Living with the Land	Future World
Spaceship Earth	Future World
Test Track	Future World
Universe of Energy	Future World

Scare Factor
! = Even your grandmother could ride this!
!! = A couple of **GOTCHA**! moments.
!!! = Serious thrills here!

Insider's Secret

EPCOT IS YOUR BIG WALKING DAY . . . LIKE FIVE TO SIX MILES. SO WEAR COMFY SHOES.

Epcot Attractions

Speed of Line	Duration of Ride/Show	Scare Factor	Cool Factor
Fast	5 min.	!!!	✔✔
Fast	20 min.	!	✔
Fast	20 min.	!	✔✔
Fast	15 min.	!	✔
Fast	25 min.	!!	✔✔✔
Fast	n/a	!	✔✔
n/a	n/a	!	✔✔✔
Fast	13 min.	!	✔
Mod	8 min.	!	✔
Fast	10 min.	!	✔
Moderate	15 min.	!	✔✔
Slow	25 min.	!!!	✔✔✔
Slow	30 min.	!	✔✔

Cool Factor
  ✔ = Totally lame!
  ✔✔ = Might be fine if you have time.
  ✔✔✔ = Don't miss this ride!

If you're not staying at a Disney hotel, either take your hotel's shuttle or drive to the Epcot parking lot and then catch a tram to the main gate.

THE BIG STUFF

Okay, two words: Test Track. This is one of the most awesome rides in all of Disney World—if not *the* most awsome—and it draws mega-lines. Your best bet is to ride it first thing in the morning, then get a FASTPASS and come back for another lap.

EPCOT ATTRACTIONS

Future World
Spaceship Earth: Spaceship Earth, a.k.a. "The Big Ball," tells the story of communications through history. The audio-animatronic robots are great, and during the ride you slowly wind your way nearly to the top of the geosphere. The final effect, where you wind down backward with a starry sky above you, is pretty cool.

"Spaceship Earth goes real slow and it's a little boring, but if you want to lean back and relax, this is the perfect place."

Hans, 16

Q&A

Q: What's the difference between a geosphere and a geodome?

A: A geodome is just the top half of the ball, but a geosphere, like Spaceship Earth, is completely round.

Universe of Energy: This show is a lot better than it used to be. Ellen DeGeneres dreams she's on *Jeopardy* and all the categories are about energy. She's losing big time until her neighbor, Bill Nye the Science Guy, shows up to help. The best part of the ride comes when your theater breaks apart and becomes a tram that takes you back to the age of the dinos. They're the biggest audio-animatronics Disney has ever created, and after riding through several scenes, you end up back where you started. Except now Ellen knows all about energy, and she's able to beat her nerdy friend Judy (played by Jamie Lee Curtis) and Einstein.

"Universe of Energy is more fun than I thought it would be. Ellen's funny."
Carolyn, 16

Journey into Imagination: This pavilion has both a ride and a 3-D movie, as well as a great interactive lab.

Honey, I Shrunk the Audience: This is a hugely funny 3-D show. You're at the Imagination Institute to see Dr. Wayne Szalinski from the movie pick up an award for Inventor of the Year. No surprise— his machine goes out of whack, and it ends up shrinking you, the audi-

Insider's Secret

AT I SHRUNK THE AUDIENCE, IF YOU'RE NOT INTO FEELING A BUNCH OF VIRTUAL MICE RUN UP YOUR LEGS, KEEP YOUR FEET IN YOUR SEAT.

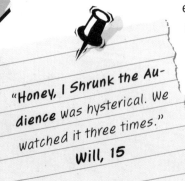

"Honey, I Shrunk the Audience was hysterical. We watched it three times."

Will, 15

ence. You face Nick Szalinski's snake, a lion, but the creepiest (really!) part is when little brother Adam's mouse gets into the machine and is multiplied 999 times.

Journey into Your Imagination: An okay, not great, ride. The idea is you're scanned by Nigel, the head of the Imagination Institute, to see what's upstairs. Turns out you've got cobwebs. So you ride through some experiments, and when it's over, you've got so much imagination that you blow the machine. Right.

ImageWorks: The best part of this cool interactive lab is "What If I Could Become Something Else?" This lets you take your picture and morph it onto a koala or a sunflower or a bunch of other things. You can e-mail the final picture home to three friends. It's fun, it's free, and if you have a bunch of friends, you can do it a bunch of times.

The Land: The Land is another pavilion with more than one thing going on. The boat ride "Listen to the Land" is really hokey and only worth doing

Insider's Secret

THE FOOD COURT IN THE LAND PAVILION HAS LOTS OF CHOICES AND IS A GOOD PLACE TO GO IF EVERYBODY CAN'T AGREE ON WHAT TO EAT.

if you're super into farming—or it's a hundred degrees outside and you're looking to crash in a cool, dark place. Circle of Life is a film about conservation, mostly for kids. Food Rocks, a fifteen-minute show with singing vegetables and fruits based on rock stars, is okay.

The Living Seas: This is an aquarium. The ride isn't much, but if you're into marine life, you can hang around as long as you want and watch the fish. The manatee are in a separate tank and they're really cute.

Test Track: This is definitely the most awesome attraction in Epcot, and maybe in all of Disney World. The idea is that you're helping GM test their new cars by volunteering to be crash dummies. Six people ride in a convertible and you test the brakes, the steering, how it reacts to heat and cold . . . then you get to the crash test. But just before you hit the wall, the doors open and

Q&A

Q: The aquarium in the Living Seas is so large that:

A. It holds more water than the wave pool at Typhoon Lagoon.

B. Spaceship Earth could float inside of it.

C. It's taller from top to bottom than Cinderella's Castle.

A: The correct answer is B.

"*Test Track* is worth doing over and over."
Andrew, 14

Ask for the front row at Test Track for the wildest ride!

you're on the outdoor track.

It's the fastest ride in Disney World, with some banks and turns built in to make it wilder—but since it doesn't flip or plunge like some of the coasters, even total weenies can handle the ride.

Insider's Secret

GET A FASTPASS AND COME BACK AT NIGHT. TEST TRACK IS EVEN MORE OF A KICK IN THE DARK.

Wonders of Life: This is another pavilion with lots going on inside. There are plenty of little inter-active exhibits, and some of them, like the exercise bikes that give you fitness feedback, are pretty cool. If you missed sex ed, you might want to check out "The Making of Me" (not), and the natural foods bar is a good place to get a snack. But the main attrac-tions of the pavilion are Body Wars, Cranium Com-mand, and Innoventions.

Body Wars: This motion-simulation ride is a whole lot rougher than Star Tours at MGM. The story is that you get miniaturized and inserted into the human body, supposedly to remove a splinter from

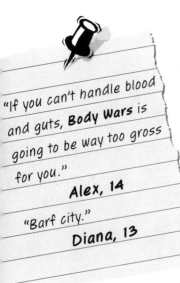

"If you can't handle blood and guts, **Body Wars** is going to be way too gross for you."
Alex, 14

"Barf city."
Diana, 13

a woman. Then—big shock—something goes wrong and you end up being swept through the bloodstream. You get bounced around like crazy as you make pit stops in the heart, lungs, and brain.

Cranium Command: This is probably the funniest show in Epcot. You're helping Fuzzy, a Cranium Command trainee, pilot the brain of a thirteen-year-old boy through a day of middle school. The right and left brain argue, the stomach complains, the bladder can't handle it, and the heart overloads at the sight of the new girl in school. You'll recognize some of the stars playing different parts of the body.

"**Cranium Command** is a funny show anyway, but all those scuzzy clothes from the early '90s just make you laugh harder."
Gaby, 16

Innoventions: Innoventions, which has two sides, is basically a big technological play area. They change the exhibits all the time, but there's always plenty of computer stuff, inventions so new they're not on the market, and virtual reality games, where you stand on a platform with a helmet on and fight bad guys or drive race cars. You'll want to spend at least thirty minutes here—longer if you're a nerd.

The World Showcase

Epcot's second section, the World Showcase, has eleven pavilions representing countries from around the world—Mexico, Norway, China, Germany, Italy, the United States, Japan, Morocco, France, the United Kingdom, and Canada. Each pavilion has shops, restaurants, live entertainment, and usually a film or small ride. The restaurants are the big deal—but the live entertainment is pretty cool, too. (Showtimes are listed on your map.) And the big closing fireworks show, IllumiNations, is reason enough to stay in Epcot until the very last minute.

Mexico: There's a cool restaurant inside the Mayan temple, where it feels like it's always night. Babyish boat ride, but an okay way to kill time while you're waiting for your food.

Norway: The boat ride has the same theme as the one in Mexico—"This is our country, don't you like

Insider's Secret

DURING THE OFF-SEASON, EPCOT IS THE ONLY PARK TO STAY OPEN AT NIGHT, USUALLY UNTIL 9 P.M., SO YOU MIGHT WANT TO GO TO ANOTHER PARK IN THE MORNING AND MOVE TO EPCOT LATER IN THE DAY.

"Norway Pavilion has the best-looking girls in Epcot."
Jeremy, 17

it?"—but with a little more excitement. You ride Viking ships, take a few little plunges, and almost go over a waterfall backward after the troll puts a whammy on you. If you want to skip the film at the end, just keep walking.

China: Chinese food (duh), a big shop with all kinds of stuff, and a 360-degree film about China. France and Canada have movies, too—you might want to see one of them, but probably not all three. The kids in the gymnastic group are great.

Germany, Italy: Food. Shops. People singing their lungs out. Keep walking.

United States: If you like American history, you'll like the show here, which uses audio-animatronic robots to pretty much give you the whole story of the United States in twenty minutes. The Civil War part is sad enough to make you cry.

Insider's Se**c**ret

AT THE U.S. PAVILION, STUFF IS GOING ON ALL OVER THE STAGE, SO THE BEST SEATS ARE IN THE MIDDLE IN THE BACK.

Japan: The drumming group is fun, and the restaurant upstairs does the Benihana thing. You know, chefs flipping shrimp tails into their hats with those Ginsu knives.

Morocco: The gymnastic troupe is amazing, especially this one guy who is so limber that he makes you sort of sick just to look at him.

France: Great places to eat and the little café in the back has tons of different kinds of pastries. Check your map for showtimes, and make sure you don't miss the Living Statues. It's a weird show—these totally unlifelike people dressed up like classical statues interact with the audience—but definitely funny and different and a great place to take pictures.

The United Kingdom: There are two great shows here: If you like retro music, a Beatles-clone group called the British Invasion plays several times a day in the little park in the back. (Your parents will get off on it even if you don't.) And the World Showcase Players do funny skits based on King Arthur in the street out front. Watch out—you might get pulled into the show.

Canada: Our vote for the best act in World Showcase is Off-Kilter, a rock group that plays totally amped-up Celtic music complete with bagpipes. Like lots of the Epcot shows, this one is hard to describe, but worth checking out. These guys are hilarious.

PARADES AND SHOWS

As listed above, street shows are going on all the time in Epcot, usually starting in the afternoon and usually in the World Showcase. But the big finale show is IllumiNations, which has incredible fireworks, lasers, music, and special effects. It's at 9 P.M. every night and worth sticking around for.

WHERE TO EAT

Epcot is all about food. You have your choice of lots of different types of restaurants, often with something funky thrown in. At the Coral Reef restaurant under the Living Seas, one whole wall is glass and you can check out the fish while you eat (although it makes you feel kinda guilty). In the Land, the

Insider's Secret

ILLUMINATIONS IS TOTALLY CROWDED, SINCE PRETTY MUCH EVERYBODY IN EPCOT SHOWS UP FOR IT. TRY AND GET YOUR PARENTS TO GET THERE EARLY AND SAVE YOU SOME SPACE AROUND THE WORLD SHOWCASE LAGOON. IF THEY'LL HOLD YOUR SEAT, THIS IS A GOOD TIME TO SNEAK ON TEST TRACK FOR ONE LAST LAP.

Garden Grille rotates and you can see scenes from inside the ride. In the World Showcase, there's a magician and a pub singer in the United Kingdom, escargot-to-go in France, the slice and dice show in Japan, PG-rated belly dancers in Morocco, yodelers at the beer hall in Germany, and the Norwegian buffet has so much strange stuff on it you probably won't recognize half of it.

Helpful Hint

Want to have dinner at a sit-down restaurant? If you're staying at a Disney hotel, you can arrange "priority seating"—Disney's term for reservations—by pushing the dining button on your phone. If you're not at a Disney hotel, look for the Dining Reservations booth to the left of Spaceship Earth as you enter in the morning.

WHERE TO SHOP

Mousegear near Innoventions is one of the biggest shops in Disney World, and they have just about everything. If you get into pin trading, the Epcot pin trading cart in Future World has a good selection. And for a really funky souvenir, check out the shops of the World Showcase. Maybe if you bring Ms. Osterwaltz back a beaded change purse from China or a collection of British teas, she'll forget all about that make-up test in Geometry.

EPCOT'S "DON'T MISS" LIST

➤ *Test Track*

➤ *Cranium Command*

➤ *Honey, I Shrunk the Audience*

➤ *Innoventions*

➤ *Universe of Energy*

➤ *The World Showcase shows, especially Off-Kilter and the Living Statues*

➤ *IllumiNations*

4

The Disney-MGM Studios

★ ★ ★ ★ ★ ★ ★ ★ ★ ★ ★ ★

According to the teenagers we talked to, MGM is definitely the best park. It's got great rides, including Rock 'n' Roller Coaster and Tower of Terror, and plenty of shows having to do with the movies. In fact, entertainment is the whole theme of MGM. They can't even serve a meal without putting on some kind of act.

HOW TO GET TO MGM

If you're staying at the Boardwalk, Yacht and Beach Club, Swan, or Dolphin, take the water taxi directly to the MGM gates. Guests of other Disney hotels take a bus.

If you're not staying at a Disney hotel, either take your hotel's shuttlebus to the park or drive.

THE BIG STUFF

Definitely, make sure you see Rock 'n' Roller Coaster, Tower of Terror, Star Tours, and the night show called Fantasmic!

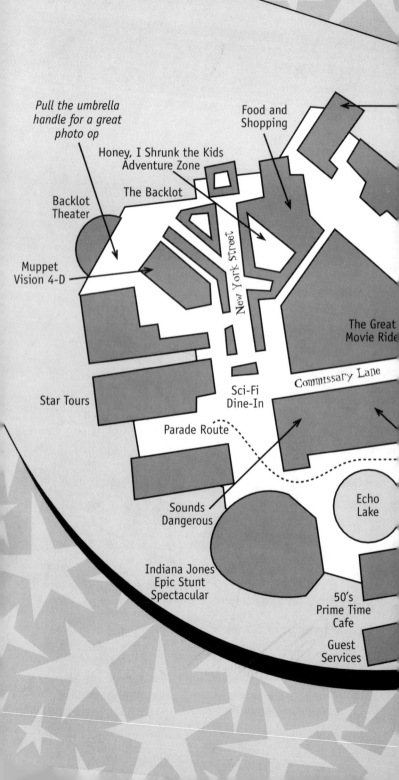

Pull the umbrella handle for a great photo op

Food and Shopping

Honey, I Shrunk the Kids Adventure Zone

The Backlot

Backlot Theater

Muppet Vision 4-D

New York Street

The Great Movie Ride

Commissary Lane

Sci-Fi Dine-In

Star Tours

Parade Route

Sounds Dangerous

Echo Lake

Indiana Jones Epic Stunt Spectacular

50's Prime Time Cafe

Guest Services

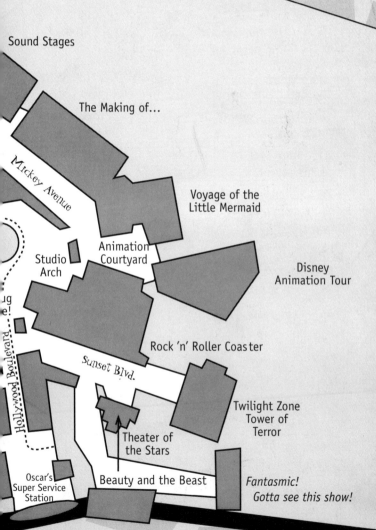

Disney-MGM Studios

Studios
Backlot Tour

Sound Stages

The Making of...

Mickey Avenue

Voyage of the
Little Mermaid

Studio
Arch

Animation
Courtyard

Disney
Animation Tour

Hollywood Boulevard

Rock 'n' Roller Coaster

Sunset Blvd.

Twilight Zone
Tower of
Terror

Theater of
the Stars

Oscar's
Super Service
Station

Beauty and the Beast

*Fantasmic!
Gotta see this show!*

ENTRANCE

Quick Guide to

Attraction	Location
The ABC Sound Studio	Hollywood Blvd.
The Backstage Pass	Mickey Ave.
Beauty and the Beast Stage Show	Sunset Blvd.
Doug Live!	Hollywood Blvd.
The Great Movie Ride	Hollywood Blvd.
The Honey, I Shrunk the Kids Adventure Zone	New York Street
The Hunchback of Notre Dame Stage Show	New York Street
The Indiana Jones Epic Stunt Spectacular	Hollywood Blvd.
The Magic of Disney Animation Tour	Animation Courtyard
The Making of . . .	Mickey Ave.
The MGM Backlot Tour	Mickey Ave.
MuppetVision 4-D	New York Street
Twilight Zone Tower of Terror	Sunset Blvd.
Rock 'n' Roller Coaster	Sunset Blvd.
Star Tours	Hollywood Blvd.
Voyage of the Little Mermaid	Animation Courtyard

Scare Factor
 ! = Even your grandmother could ride this!
 ‼ = A couple of **GOTCHA**! moments.
 ‼! = Serious thrills here!

MGM Attractions

Speed of Line	Duration of Ride/Show	Scare Factor	Cool Factor
Slow	15 min.	!!	✔✔
Fast	25 min.	!	✔
Fast	30 min.	!	✔✔
Moderate	17 min.	!	✔
Fast	2.5 min.	!!	✔✔✔
Slow	as long as you like	!	✔
Fast	30 min.	!	✔
Fast	30 min	!	✔✔✔
Moderate	35 min.	!	✔✔
Fast	25 min.	!	✔
Fast	35 min.	!	✔✔
Fast	20 min.	!!	✔✔✔
Fast	10 min.	!!!	✔✔✔
Moderate	3 min.	!!!	✔✔✔
Moderate	10 min.	!!	✔✔✔
Slow	20 min.	!	✔✔

Cool Factor
  ✔ = Totally lame!
  ✔✔ = Might be fine if you have time.
  ✔✔✔ = Don't miss this ride!

FunFactoid

Rod Serling had been dead many years when he "narrated" the Tower of Terror preshow. Disney spliced together a bunch of old clips of *The Twilight Zone*, sometimes a word at a time.

MGM ATTRACTIONS

Tower of Terror: Many people (including one of your fearless authors) will tell you this is the best attraction in Walt Disney World. Maybe people love it because it's a show and a ride all in one; you can't compare it to the raise-and-drop rides at other theme parks because there's so much else going on.

The ride takes place in a big old falling-down hotel from the 1930s where one night five people—a movie star couple, a child star, her nanny, and the bellboy—got in an elevator. The story is told in

"*Tower of Terror* is like nothing else, and there's no way you could ride it just once. My mom loved it and she hates most roller coaster-type rides."

Brittany, 14

"*Tower of Terror* was one hot ride. I had to go on it twice because I had my eyes closed the first time."

Matt, 17

a creepy black-and-white film narrated by the host of the old *Twilight Zone* TV show, Rod Serling. Anyway, a bolt of lightning hit the hotel, the elevator dropped, and all the people were transported into the twilight zone.

Now it's your turn to get on the elevator. You make a couple of stops on the way up to see special effects, like holographic images of the five lost people trying to get you to join them, but of course the real point of the ride is at the end, when your elevator cage is dropped thirteen stories. You plunge faster than free-fall—which means that if you hold a penny in the palm of your hand, you'll land before the penny. Then they haul you up and do it again. And again. Then one more time. It's called a bungee pattern.

Helpful Hint

Don't freak out because the TV ads for Tower of Terror show you standing up during the elevator plunge. Yeah right. In real life you're sitting down with a lap bar.

Rock 'n' Roller Coaster: MGM's newest ride flips. Three times to be exact, two barrels and one head-over-heels. And that's the tame part.

The story is that you're Aerosmith fans who

Scare Factor

At Rock 'n' Roller Coaster, raise your hands for the take-off. Not only will you be slammed by G-forces, but you'll look cool in the picture.

"Rock 'n' Roller Coaster is the best ride in Disney World."

Ethan, 16

"Most coasters scare me but this one doesn't go very high. If you look, you can see it's all inside a building."

Amanda, 13

have come to watch them record. They're running late for a show in L.A., but they refuse to go without you, their loyal fans, so their manager hires a "really fast" stretch limo to take you all to the concert. After this short preshow, you enter a room that's like a back alley and wait for your limo.

The wildest part of the ride is the very beginning when the limo accelerates from 0 to 60 in three seconds and leads you right into your first flip. (You're moving so fast that for a second your lips actually *look* like Steven Tyler's.) You'll be zipping around the freeways of L.A., with Aerosmith music blasting all around you, and at one point you go through the 0 in the "Hollywood" sign. Within two minutes you're pulling up backstage for the concert.

Helpful Hint

Ride Rock 'n' Roller Coaster first thing after you get to MGM because the lines can get long. Then get a FASTPASS and come back.

Star Tours: George Lucas was creative consultant on this ride, and it really is a lot like being in a *Star Wars* movie. It's a motion-simulation ride where your crazy droid pilot (played by Pee Wee Herman) is supposed to take you to the Moon of Endor but screws up; you end up in the middle of an intergalactic combat zone. There's lots of bouncing around and incredible visual effects.

Even waiting to board is great for *Star Wars* fans, since you see R2-D2, C-3PO, and Admiral Ackbar in line, and if you listen carefully, you might hear them paging Egroeg Sacul (George Lucas). Sometimes characters like Chewbacca are walking around hanging out with the tourists.

The gift shop as you exit is another gotta-see for fans of the movies. Outside, at night, you can sometimes hear the Ewoks in the Ewok village, and on hot days the AT-AT blows water at you.

Beauty and the Beast: If you loved the movie, you'll love this show. It has all the music and costumes and dancing of the Broadway play, but it's a lot shorter—and it's free. Most of the showtimes are in the afternoon, so you might like the chance to sit down and rest for thirty minutes.

"I loved the part in *Beauty and the Beast* where they released the doves at the end."

Elyce, 16

Helpful Hint

The Beauty and the Beast theater is near Tower of Terror and Rock 'n' Roller Coaster, so your friends who are too scared to ride those can catch a show and meet you later.

"The grand finale of the Great Movie Ride, with all the clips from movies, is my favorite part of the ride."

Leigh, 15

The Great Movie Ride: If you're a movie freak, get in line now! This ride is in the Chinese Theater at the end of Hollywood Boulevard. The stars' handprints and footprints are in the concrete pavement outside, and while you're waiting to board, you'll see things like Dorothy's ruby slippers and a carousel horse from Mary Poppins, as well as clips from great old movies.

The ride itself takes you through scenes from classic movies, and at one point you'll either meet (depending on what car you happen to be in) a gangster on the run from the cops or a cowboy trying to escape John Wayne. The bad guy will kick out your tram driver and take over your tram, which is pretty interesting, especially if you're sitting up front and the bad guy can kid around with you and try to take your jewelry.

MuppetVision 3-D: This show is so funny that it's surpassed its name and now is jokingly called MuppetVision 4-D. The preshow is one of the best parts of the whole thing, so don't talk through it, and read all the stuff written on signs and the walls. Half the jokes are hidden.

Once in the theater, you see a hilarious film with great 3-D effects. This is the kind of show any age person will find funny, from your little sister to your granny. Stuff goes on all around you; be sure to turn around to look at the Swedish Chef when he's talking, especially at the end.

Sounds Dangerous at the ABC Sound Studio: Drew Carey plays an undercover cop in this show, which is mostly about sound effects. It's amazing how much of the story you can figure out just based on what you hear—but you sit in darkness for a couple of minutes, and this always seems to freak out some kid who screams through the rest of the show, spoiling it for everybody.

Indiana Jones Epic Stunt Spectacular!: Stunt doubles recreate action scenes from the *Indiana Jones* movies, showing you how everything was done. It's loud, wild, and—since they pull out audience volunteers who don't know what's going on—funny, too. Some of the stunts are really dangerous—that exploding sound you hear every so often as you're walking around MGM is the Indiana Jones crew blowing up the Nazi plane right on stage.

Insider's Secret

WANT TO BE A STUNT DOUBLE? SHOW UP EARLY FOR INDIANA JONES . . . THEY PULL VOLUNTEERS FROM THE FRONT OF THE LINE.

Animation Tour: Artists shouldn't miss this excellent tour. The opening film with Robin Williams and Walter Cronkite sets up the whole idea of how animation can make you feel different emotions. Next you get to walk through the studios and see the artists working on scenes for an upcoming Disney movie. The best part is when an animator shows the tour group how to draw a character. The animators are so fast it's unbelievable. Then you watch a wrap-up movie about Disney animated hits.

Helpful Hint

Ride the rides in the morning before the park gets too crowded. Save the tours and shows for the afternoon.

Voyage of the Little Mermaid: Like Beauty and the Beast . . . if you loved the movie, you'll love the show. Most of the special effects involve puppets and water. The theater's kinda small and lines get really long; if you're there on a crowded day, do Beauty and the Beast instead.

"I got dragged into all of th kiddie movie shows because of my little sister. I liked them better than I expected, especially **Little Mermaid**."
Christina, 14

Helpful Hint

Little Mermaid has a FASTPASS during the on-season. It definitely saves time, since every kid in the park lines up for this show.

Insider's Secret

ONE OF THE BEST PHOTO OPS IN MGM IS NEAR THE HUNCHBACK THEATER. SEE THAT UMBRELLA HANGING ON A LAMPPOST? GIVE IT A PULL AND WATER COMES DOWN AROUND YOU, JUST LIKE IN THE OLD MOVIE SINGING IN THE RAIN.

The Hunchback of Notre Dame: In this case, the show is more fun than the movie, but it's never as crowded as Beauty and the Beast or Little Mermaid, so it's a good choice if you just want to sit down and rest for thirty minutes in the afternoon.

Insider's Secret

WANT TO GET WET AT CATASTROPHE CANYON? SIT ON THE LEFT SIDE OF THE TRAM.

Backlot Tour: If you're into behind-the-scenes info on moviemaking, this is the tour for you. You ride through costuming departments and outdoor sets. The best part is Catastrophe Canyon, where they re-create a flood right before your eyes. The tour takes about forty minutes, though, so only do it if you have plenty of time.

Other MGM Attractions: Doug Live! is a musical stage show that's mostly for kids. The "Honey, I Shrunk the Kids" play area is also for rugrats, but a great place to take pictures, especially if you pose inside the roll of Kodak film. Backstage Pass and "The Making of . . ." are worth your time only if you really liked the film they're talking about. Otherwise, they're both a big snooze.

Q&A

Q: What do Britney Spears, Christina Aguilera, and Justin Timberlake of 'N Sync have in common?

A: They all got their show biz start on the Mickey Mouse Club.

PARADES AND SHOWS

There's a short parade every day around 3 P.M. that features whatever Disney movie has just come out. Sometimes if they have a "Celebrity of the Day," they'll do a parade for that, too, which can be pretty exciting if you know the celeb. These parades end in front of the Chinese Theater, where the star does the whole hand-print and footprint thing.

But the big deal show is the nighttime finale called "Fantasmic!" This is probably the best Disney closing show anywhere, beating out even IllumiNations for sheer fire power. The theme is good vs. evil with poor little Mickey having to fight off every bad guy who has ever been in a Disney movie. Unbelievable special effects, especially when they project movie scenes onto a wall of water, and the show might have you crying by the end. It's that emotional.

"If you sit up front at Fantasmic!, you'll get wet."

Paul, 13

Helpful Hint

Everybody in the whole park (and it feels like everybody in the world) shows up for Fantasmic!, so get there at least an hour early for a good seat. You can bring in food and eat if you don't want to waste time, and the preshow is pretty good. It's one of the few places where you'll hear Disney making fun of itself.

WHERE TO EAT

MGM is full of great restaurants; they have so much going on you might forget to actually eat. The Prime Time Café is a hoot, since the idea is that you're in an old sitcom and the waitress is your mother. She keeps yelling at you about your homework, and getting your bike out of the driveway, and eating your peas. The S'More's are an awesome dessert.

Another fun place is the Sci-Fi Dine-In, where you eat in cars and watch hokey clips from those old horror movies where all the monsters are wrapped in tin foil and chasing girls with really bad hairdos. The Hollywood Brown Derby is elegant and has the best food in the park, but it's expensive, so only go if your parents are buying. Mama Melrose's has good pizza, or you could hit any of the fast-food places. The Backlot Express, near Star Tours, is the fastest.

WHERE TO SHOP

MGM has all the standard Disney souvenirs in the stores along Hollywood Boulevard, but you can also get Indiana Jones stuff (need a whip, anybody?), Muppet stuff, and Star Wars stuff in the shops located as you exit the rides. The shop as you leave Tower of Terror has towels and ashtrays from the Hollywood Tower Hotel, where the ride takes place, and you can get presents for rock 'n' rollers as you exit the Rock 'n' Roller Coaster.

Into the bad guys? Check out Villains in Vogue on Sunset Boulevard.

MGM "DON'T MISS" LIST

★ Tower of Terror

★ Rock 'n' Roller Coaster

★ Star Tours

★ Muppetvision 4-D

★ The Great Movie Ride

★ Indiana Jones Epic Stunt Spectacular!

★ Fantasmic!

And hey, if you want to go see the Belle or Ariel show, we won't tell anybody.

CHAPTER 5

Animal Kingdom

The Animal Kingdom seems like it's the smallest park because there are not that many rides and shows. But it's really the biggest . . . five hundred acres with over two thousand animals.

GETTING TO THE ANIMAL KINGDOM

Not a lot of options here. If you're staying in a Disney resort, take a bus. If you're not staying in a Disney hotel, either take a bus from your off-site hotel or drive your car.

Insider's Secret

SINCE THERE AREN'T THAT MANY RIDES, YOU CAN DO THE ANIMAL KINGDOM IN FOUR OR FIVE HOURS.

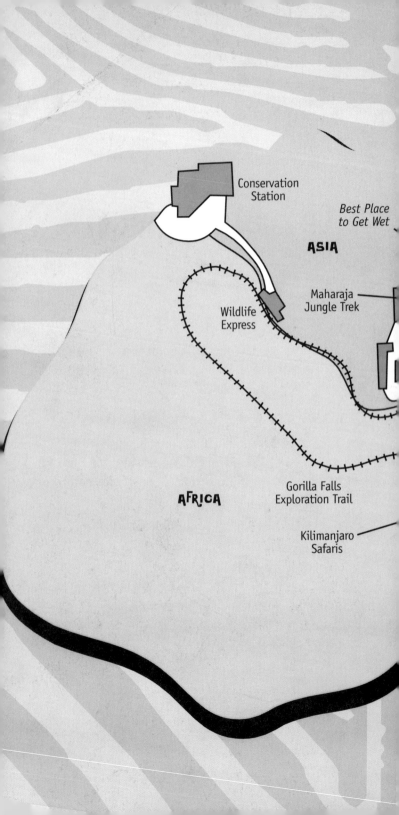

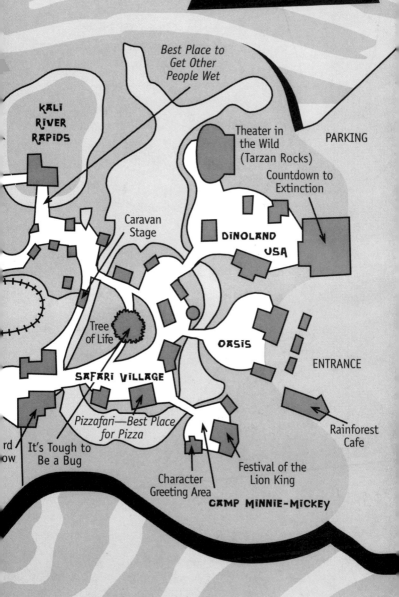

Animal Kingdom

KALI RIVER RAPIDS

Best Place to Get Other People Wet

Theater in the Wild (Tarzan Rocks)

PARKING

Countdown to Extinction

Caravan Stage

DINOLAND USA

Tree of Life

OASIS

ENTRANCE

SAFARI VILLAGE

Pizzafari—Best Place for Pizza

rd ow

It's Tough to Be a Bug

Rainforest Cafe

Character Greeting Area

Festival of the Lion King

CAMP MINNIE-MICKEY

Quick Guide to

Attraction	Location
Countdown to Extinction	Dinoland
Festival of the Lion King	Camp Minnie-Mickey
Gorilla Falls Exploration Trail	Africa
Grandmother Willow's Grove	Camp Minnie-Mickey
Kali River Rapids	Asia
Kilimanjaro Safaris	Africa
Maharajah Jungle Trek	Asia
Tarzan Rocks! at Theater in the Wild	Dinoland
The Tree of Life, featuring *It's Tough to Be a Bug*	Safari Village
Wildlife Express to Conservation Station	Africa

Scare Factor
  ! = Even your grandmother could ride this!
  !! = A couple of **GOTCHA**! moments.
  !!! = Serious thrills here!

THE BiG STUFF

The big-deal rides are Countdown to Extinction, Kilimanjaro Safaris, and Kali River Rapids. (All of them offer a FASTPASS on busy days.) Shows that draw big crowds are the 3-D film "It's Tough to Be a Bug," Festival of the Lion King, and Tarzan Rocks!

Animal Kingdom Attractions

Speed of Line	Duration of Ride/Show	Scare Factor	Cool Factor
Moderate	10 min.	!!!	✔✔✔
Moderate	25 min.	!	✔✔✔
Moderate	10 min.	!	✔
Fast	12 min.	!	✔
Fast	30 min.	!	✔✔
Moderate	7 min.	!!	✔✔✔
Moderate	20 min.	!!	✔✔✔
Fast	1–0 min.	!	✔✔
Slow	8 min.	!!	✔✔✔
Fast	10 min.	!	✔

Cool Factor
✔ = Totally lame!
✔✔ = Might be fine if you have time.
✔✔✔ = Don't miss this ride!

ANIMAL KINGDOM ATTRACTIONS

"It's Tough to Be a Bug" (Inside the Tree of Life): Like "Honey, I Shrunk the Kids" in Epcot, this very funny show uses physical effects, not just visual ones. The concept is that humans are always trying to wipe out the pitiful little bugs of the world and now they're getting their revenge. At a couple of points in the show you might want to seriously watch your back, and the stinkbug is . . . real authentic.

"Stay seated as 'It's **Tough to be a Bug**' is ending. The final effect is hilarious."
Shannon, 17

Insider's Secret

THE LINE FOR "IT'S TOUGH TO BE A BUG" WINDS ALL AROUND THE TREE OF LIFE, SO THIS IS A GREAT TIME TO LOOK AT ALL THE ANIMAL CARVINGS IN THE TREE TRUNK.

Q&A

Q: What's the biggest animal in the Tree of Life trunk?

A: The blue whale.

Kilimanjaro Safaris: You'll feel like your Jeep is going through an African animal reserve, but it's actually all on Disney property. The animals roam free—with a few fences hidden among the trees and bushes—and even cross the path that your Jeep will follow. The story line is that you're helping the reserve's game warden look for poachers who have stolen a baby elephant, Little Red, but it's all really just an excuse to drive fast at the end.

The safari is a great place to take pictures, but think twice about videotaping; it can get pretty bumpy, and your tape will come out looking like the *Blair Witch Project.* How many animals you see is pretty much a matter of luck, but a good time to ride is right after it rains, or first thing in the morning. The animals like to come out and explore when it cools off a bit. If you go in the middle of the day, they'll probably be napping.

"The safari ride was the best part of the Animal Kingdom. When we passed the rocks where the lions are, the male was standing right on the edge of a cliff just like Simba in the movie poster. My whole family went nuts."

Eric, 13

Q&A

Q: How do you tell a crocodile from an alligator?

A: The crocodile has a narrow jaw, a pointed snout, and two of his lower teeth stick out even when his mouth is closed.

Q: A monkey from an ape?

A: A monkey has a tail, an ape usually does not.

Q: Chip from Dale?

A: Chip's nose is brown (think "chocolate chip") and Dale's nose is red.

Gorilla Falls Exploration Trail: The beginning of this path is right outside of Kilimanjaro Safaris, and leads through preserves with African animals. Unless you're really into gorillas, you might want to skip it. But if you loved *The Lion King,* then stop to see the warthogs and meerkats in the Pumbaa and Timon exhibit. The meerkats are pretty cute.

FunFactoid

On the **Gorilla Falls Exploration Trail,**
keep an eye out for Gino, the silverback
gorilla. The dominant male in each troop
is called a silverback because he's usually
older and has gray hair mixed in with black.

Insider's Secret

A GREAT PHOTO OP IS THE OPEN ANIMAL CARGO CRATE TO YOUR RIGHT JUST AS YOU LEAVE KILIMANJARO SAFARIS. GET YOUR FRIENDS TO POSE INSIDE.

Wildlife Express to Conservation Station: The train is cool-looking, but once you get to Conservation Station, there's not much to do. Very skippable.

Countdown to Extinction: The set-up? You're at this high-tech museum that offers field trips back to the Cretaceous period. The real story? A rebel scientist has reset your coordinates so that you can help him save the iguanadon (a gentle vegetarian dinosaur) from extinction. One slight problem . . . saving the iguanadon requires traveling back in time to a point where an asteroid hit the earth, so you've got to grab your dino and get out of there fast. Another problem . . . not all the dinosaurs you meet along the way are vegetarians.

"Awesome! Countdown to Extinction is the best ride in the Animal Kingdom!!"
Chandy, 15

Countdown to Extinction is definitely worth riding twice—the first time through you'll be trying so hard to hang on that you'll miss half the dinosaurs.

Scare Factor

To really feel the Jeep's movement at Countdown to Extinction, choose an outside seat. The smoothest ride is in the front and center.

Insider's Secret

AT COUNTDOWN TO EXTINCTION, WHEN THE T-REX ROARS, SAY CHEESE!

Theater in the Wild: The current feature is Tarzan Rocks!, but the shows here change on a regular basis.

Tarzan Rocks! has great rollerblading stunts and an aerial ballet starring Tarzan and Jane. The live band that plays songs from the movie is good, but it's not the most exciting show in the Animal Kingdom, so skip it if you're short on time.

Festival of the Lion King: One of the best shows in any Disney park. This twenty-five-minute performance doesn't let up once . . . the costumes are incredible, the music's great, and all the *Lion King* characters show up. There are also some great gymnastics starring the Tumble-monkeys, an aerial ballet featuring a girl in a bird costume, and even a guy twirling fire batons.

Q: What's a sleeper?

A: A ride or show that the Imagineers didn't expect to be as popular as it became. When the Animal Kingdom opened, the Disney people were shocked to see monster lines outside Festival of the Lion King. They expanded the theater . . . but the lines are still long!

Insider's Secret

ACCORDING TO TUMBLE-MONKEY RIC, THE BEST SEAT IN THE HOUSE AT FESTIVAL OF THE LION KING IS IN THE BACK ROW OF THE WARTHOG SECTION.

Pocahontas Show (in Grandmother Willow's Grove): This show features Pocahontas and Grandmother Willow, as well as some live animals they've trained to do simple tricks. The message is that we should all work together to save the forest and the creatures who live there. Cute for kids, but if you're deciding between this and Countdown to Extinction . . . well, that's an obvious choice.

Kali River Rapids: Eight people get into a circular raft and descend down a river full of rapids. The theme is ecology and how too much logging is ruining the rainforest. At least that's what they say the theme is. The real theme is "How wet can you get?"

There's only one big dip near the end, but the huge fountain near the beginning is likely to get you

> "The rafts at **Kali River Rapids** are circular and make lots of turns as they go through the fountains and waterfalls, so there's no way of telling who's going to get it."
>
> **Brennon, 17**

> "If you ride **Kali River Rapids** early in the morning before the crowd gets bad, they'll let you stay on and go through again."
>
> **Nola, 15**

soaked. Which is a lot of fun in the summer, but not quite as big a kick at 10 A.M. in January. So unless you're in Animal Kingdom on a really hot day, save Kali River Rapids for the afternoon. Make sure you take off your watch and leave anything like cameras or camcorders in the lockers near

Helpful Hint

Some people bring rain ponchos or big trash bags just for Kali River Rapids. If you were planning on buying a T-shirt at the Animal Kingdom, you'll probably want to buy it after this.

Insider's Secret

WATER CANNONS ARE LOCATED ON THE BRIDGE JUST AS YOU EXIT KALI RIVER RAPIDS. STOP AND TAKE AIM AT THE PEOPLE IN THE RAFTS GOING BY.

the beginning of the ride. And most important of all, put your shoes in the central bin and keep your feet up on the railing. A wet butt just makes you itchy; wet shoes and socks can give you blisters and wreck your whole day.

Flights of Wonder: This is an okay bird show. Only stop if you're a bird fanatic. If not, move on.

Maharajah Jungle Trek: If you only have time to take one walking path, choose this one over Gorilla Falls Exploration Trail because the Asian animals are more unusual than the African ones. You'll see Bengal tigers, Komodo dragons, and gibbons.

"Maharajah Jungle Trek is a great place to hang out and stay dry if your friends are riding Kali River Rapids next door and you don't want to get wet."

Marianne, 14

River Cruise with Radio Disney: Like the music and games of Radio Disney? Check out this boat ride around the Tree of Life. Radio Disney DJs Mark and Zippy are your hosts. The lines can get pretty long for what is basically a simple cruise. Only open during summer and holiday weeks.

WHERE TO EAT

Not a lot of choices—the Rainforest Café is the only sit-down restaurant in the whole park. We think Tusker House Restaurant in the Africa section has the best food in the Animal Kingdom, with great salads, great beef and chicken kebabs and yummy desserts.

Insider's Secret

THE ANIMAL KINGDOM HAS FEWER PLACES TO EAT THAN THE OTHER DISNEY PARKS, AND LINES AT LUNCH CAN GET REALLY LONG. JUST GET A SNACK FROM A FAST-FOOD PLACE OR HAVE LUNCH AFTER YOU EXIT THE PARK.

WHERE TO SHOP

The Animal Kingdom has the best stuffed animals of any park, since you can get Mickey, Minnie, and the gang in safari gear. (Our fave is Eeyore, who's carrying the tent on his back.) The T-shirts are different from those in the other parks, too. The best selection is at Beastly Bazaar or Island Merchandile.

ANIMAL KINGDOM "DON'T MISS" LIST

- 🐾 Countdown to Extinction
- 🐾 Kilimanjaro Safaris
- 🐾 "It's Tough to Be a Bug"
- 🐾 Kali River Rapids
- 🐾 Festival of the Lion King

Insider's Secret

SINCE IT DOESN'T TAKE A WHOLE DAY TO DO THE ANIMAL KINGDOM AND THERE ISN'T A BIG CLOSING SHOW, MOST PEOPLE LEAVE THE PARK IN THE AFTERNOON. THIS IS A GOOD TIME TO STOP AT BLIZZARD BEACH, WHICH IS LOCATED CLOSE BY AND SHARES BUSES WITH THE ANIMAL KINGDOM.

The Rest of the World

⊙ ⊙ ⊙ ⊙ ⊙ ⊙ ⊙ ⊙ ⊙ ⊙

If there were only the four big theme parks, Disney just wouldn't be Disney. Some of the best times you'll have will be at Disney's "minor" parks, especially the water parks. There are three complete water parks in Disney World, not counting the great hotel pools, and they've gotten better as they've gone along.

GETTiNG TO THE REST OF THE WORLD

Disney hotels run buses to the two major water parks, Typhoon Lagoon and Blizzard Beach. The easiest way to River Country is to go to the Magic Kingdom and take the launch boat from there. Disney hotels also run buses to Downtown Disney. To get to the Wide World of Sports, take a bus to the TTC and transfer there.

If you're not staying at a Disney hotel, you'll probably have to drive. Hardly any non-Disney hotels run shuttles to the minor parks.

1. Coronado Springs Resort
2. Wide World of Sports
3. Swan Resort
4. Dolphin Resort
5. Yacht & Beach Club Resorts
6. Disney's BoardWalk
7. Magic Kingdom Main Entrance
8. Car Care Center
9. Transportation & Ticket Center Parking
10. Transportation & Ticket Center
11. Polynesian Resort
12. The Grand Floridian
13. Contemporary Resort
14. Wilderness Lodge
15. Fort Wilderness Campground
16. Dixie Landings Resort
17. Port Orleans Resort
18. Old Key West Resort
19. Lake Buena Vista Golf Course
20. Disney Institute
21. Disney Institute Villas
22. Disney's West Side
23. Pleasure Island
24. Caribbean Beach Resort
25. Animal Kingdom Lodge
26. Disney Village Hotels
27. All-Star Resorts

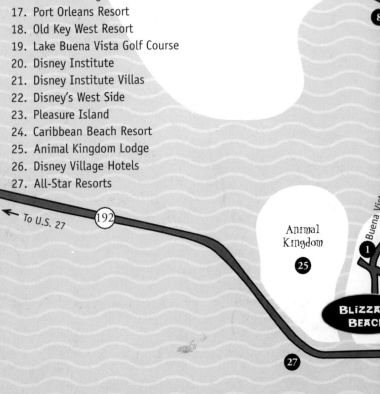

Which Water Park is Right for You?

The most important thing in a water park is:
   A. The slides
   B. The waves
   C. The pools

Long lines are:
   A. Part of the deal. This is Disney World, after all.
   B. Okay only if it's a big deal ride.
   C. A major pain.

I like to lie by the pool with:
   A. Who has time to lie by the pool?
   B. Plenty of sunscreen and one of those umbrella fruity drinks.
   C. A big old shade tree and a slice of watermelon.

The number one thing I'm looking for is:
   A. Thrills
   B. Spills
   C. The chance to chill

Mostly A's? Hit the slopes of Blizzard Beach.
Mostly B's? There's a wave with your name on it at Typhoon Lagoon.
Mostly C's? Are you sure you're a teenager? Get your inner tube and wade into River Country.

BLIZZARD BEACH

Blizzard Beach has Summit Plummet, the longest water slide in the world. The real world, not just the Disney one. It also has plenty of other slides, and the coolest (really) theme of any water park.

The idea is that a freak snowstorm hit Florida and a bunch of businessmen decided to build a ski lodge. The sun came out, the snow melted, and they're thinking their money is going to wash away with it. Then they see this alligator using the ski slopes like a giant slip-and-slide, and that's how Blizzard Beach was born. (The alligator is still around as the park mascot; they call him Ice Gator.)

You can take a ski lift to the top of Mount Rushmore, the big hill in the middle of the park, but how you get down is pretty much up to you. Summit Plummet is 120 feet tall with a killer

"Cross your legs before you go down **Summit Plummet**. You'll know why in about two seconds."

Kyle, 17

Scare Factor

Summit Plummet has the highest height requirement in all of Disney. You're going faster than the cars at Space Mountain!

Q&A

Q: What goes faster?

A. A rocket ship on Space Mountain

B. A Telejeep in Countdown to Extinction

C. Your body on Summit Plummet

A: The correct answer is C. You can reach speeds of 55 mph—so listen to Kyle and cross your legs!

60-degree drop. Slush Gusher is another big-deal slide, but it's got a couple of bumps built in to slow you down.

We really love Teamboat Springs, the whitewater raft ride. The heavier the raft, the faster you'll go, so get the whole group aboard and hang on. The inner tube rides are called Runoff Rapids, and there are three differ-ent routes down. (The enclosed tube is defi-nitely the wild-est. Scream inside of this and your head will be ringing for days.) Downhill Double Dipper is another tube ride, this one so fast that you freefall for two seconds.

The two sledding routes are also great. In Tobog-gan Racers, eight people line up for a straight race to the bottom of the mountain. (The "race" is just

> "We were just going to go by **Blizzard Beach** for a couple of hours and ended up staying all day. You look at the number of rides and think it won't take long, but they're so great you end up doing all of them more than once."
>
> Lisa, 16

Helpful Hint

Take lots of breaks at the water parks. Unless you're willing to wait for the poky chairlift every time, you'll end up climbing thousands of steps a day. It's 157 steps just to the top of Runoff Rapids, so the water parks are a lot more tiring than just walking around the theme parks.

kind of a gimmick, since the heaviest person always wins.) Snow Stormers is a slalom run, with three different twisting paths you take down on your belly.

For littler kids there's the Ski Patrol Training Camp, with miniversions of the big deal slides, and Tike's Peak for the toddlers. Anybody can hop on an inner tube and circle the park on Cross Country Creek. Melt Away Bay is the wave pool, but it's pathetic in comparison to the mondo pool at Typhoon Lagoon. If you're really into bodysurfing, go to Typhoon.

Helpful Hint

Admission to the water parks is included in Park Hopper Plus passes. Otherwise, it's $28. Ouch.

Typhoon Lagoon

Until Blizzard Beach opened, Typhoon Lagoon was the biggest water park in the world, and some teens still prefer it. There aren't as many slides, but the pool area is the best, and some people just prefer the idea of being stranded on a tropical island in a *Gilligan's Island* sort of way.

Insider's Secret

HARDLY ANYBODY IS AWARE OF THIS, BUT YOU CAN EVEN TAKE SURFING LESSONS AT TYPHOON LAGOON BEFORE THE PARK OPENS. CALL 407-WDW-SURF FOR TIMES, PRICES, AND DETAILS.

The attraction here is the 2.5-acre surfing lagoon, where machine-made waves can reach six feet high. The Disney people run different patterns, depending on the hour; sometimes you just bob around in tubes, and sometimes they get all the tubes and the kids out and crank up the wave machine for bodysurfing. A foghorn blast lets you know when a major wave is on its way.

Just because Typhoon Lagoon is known as the surfing park doesn't mean there aren't slides. Humunga Kowabunga looks plenty huge to anybody who hasn't seen Summit Plummet, and you reach speeds of 30 mph. Storm Slides are great winding slides, and the two tube slides, Keelhaul Falls and Mayday Falls, are fun, too. The whitewater ride, Gangplank Falls, is a major snooze in contrast to the much bigger and faster Teamboat Springs at Blizzard Beach.

At Shark Reef you go into a saltwater tank with snorkels, and the sharks are behind Plexiglas, so it sort of looks like you're swimming with them. Underline "sort of." The sharks are small and there aren't too many of them, so it's not like you're auditioning for *Jaws* or anything.

Insider's Secret

IF YOU'RE A GIRL, A ONE-PIECE BATHING SUIT IS YOUR BEST BET. ACCORDING TO THE GUYS WHO WORK THE MAJOR WATER SLIDES, AT LEAST ONE GIRL PER HOUR LOSES HER BIKINI TOP.

IF YOU'RE A BOY, YOU MIGHT WANT TO PAY ATTENTION TO THE TIP ABOVE.

You can rest by hopping an inner tube and circling the park on Castaway Creek, and there's Ketchakiddie Creek for the little kids.

RIVER COUNTRY

River Country is the smallest and oldest of the Disney water parks, and most of it is built into a bay, not a pool. So you're pretty much swimming in lake water. They've got nets for critter control, but this is not the day to wear your new $80 bathing suit.

Think Tom Sawyer and Huck Finn sneaking off for the day. They've got swing ropes, a couple of small water slides, and one inner-tube ride down a long creek called White Water Rapids. Which is hard to figure, because the water isn't white and it sure isn't rapid. In short, this park is more for little kids who are into splashing around and jumping off rocks.

Insider's Secret

THE BEST THING ABOUT RIVER COUNTRY IS THE LOCATION. IF YOU'RE AT THE MAGIC KINGDOM ON A REALLY HOT DAY, YOU CAN BRING A BATHING SUIT OR WEAR IT UNDER YOUR CLOTHES. AFTER LUNCH, TAKE THE LAUNCH TO RIVER COUNTRY AND SWIM FOR A COUPLE OF HOURS. IT'S A GREAT WAY TO COOL OFF, AND AS LONG AS YOU HAVE A PARK HOPPER PLUS PASS, IT'S FREE.

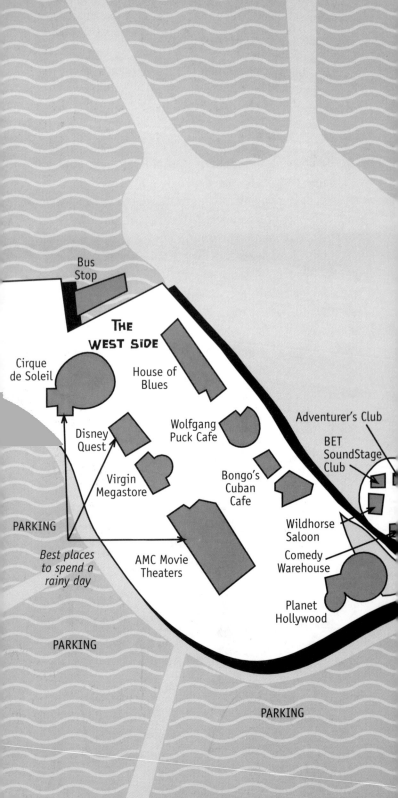

Bus
Stop

THE
WEST SIDE

Cirque
de Soleil

House of
Blues

Wolfgang
Puck Cafe

Adventurer's Club

BET
SoundStage
Club

Disney
Quest

Virgin
Megastore

Bongo's
Cuban
Cafe

Wildhorse
Saloon

PARKING

Comedy
Warehouse

*Best places
to spend a
rainy day*

AMC Movie
Theaters

Planet
Hollywood

PARKING

PARKING

Downtown Disney and Pleasure Island

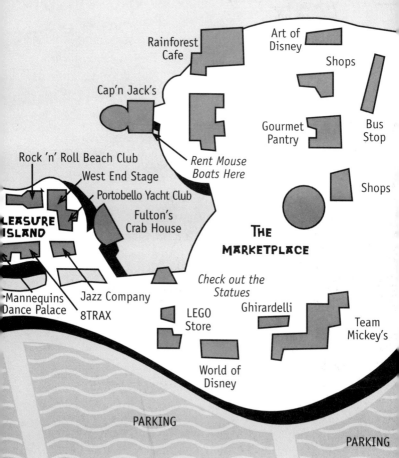

Disney Institute

Rainforest Cafe

Art of Disney

Shops

Cap'n Jack's

Gourmet Pantry

Bus Stop

Rent Mouse Boats Here

Rock 'n' Roll Beach Club

West End Stage

Portobello Yacht Club

Shops

Fulton's Crab House

PLEASURE ISLAND

THE MARKETPLACE

Mannequins Dance Palace

Jazz Company

8TRAX

Check out the Statues

LEGO Store

Ghirardelli

Team Mickey's

World of Disney

PARKING

PARKING

DOWNTOWN DiSNEY

Downtown Disney is a huge restaurant, shops, and entertainment complex divided into three parts: the Marketplace, Pleasure Island, and West Side.

Downtown Disney Marketplace

Lots of shopping here—it's like a Disney-themed strip mall with a store devoted to Disney art, one to sporting gear, another for home decorating stuff, one for Christmas ornaments, and somewhere or another they sell pretty much anything you can imagine that can be shaped into mouse ears. World of Disney, the biggest Disney store on the planet, is a good place to start, especially if you've promised about a hundred people at home you'll bring them something. You'll find everything from $3,000 Rolex watches to a pack of eight Goofy tattoos for $3.

Another store worth checking out is the Lego Superstore. The Lego statues outside, including life-size dinosaurs and a sea serpent, are just incredible.

Pleasure Island

You can't go here. Literally. These nightclubs are open only to people over twenty-one, although you can go into the comedy club with your parents. There are a few shops and places to eat, and if you want to just see the clubs (all of which have their own individual themes, everything from a country-and-western bar to a '70s disco called 8-TRAX), you can walk through in the afternoon before they open and check everything out. If you do, be sure to stop at the Adventurer's Club. It's where Indiana Jones would go to have a beer, and the T-shirts are the best, too.

West Side

Most of the better restaurants are on the West Side: Planet Hollywood, Bongo's Cuban Café, the House of Blues, and the Wolfgang Puck Café, to name a few. If

Helpful Hint

The West Side restaurants don't take advance reservations, but they'll give you a beeper so you can walk around looking at stuff while you wait. The best time to come is early . . . around 5 P.M.

you're planning on eating here, it'll be expensive. But that's not your problem, right?

There's also plenty of entertainment on the West Side. Cirque du Soleil and DisneyQuest (see below) are here, as well as an ice skating rink, a twenty-four-screen AMC movie theater, and a Virgin Megastore. On weekends they frequently have street concerts. If you can't find something to do, you're just not trying.

DisneyQuest: DisneyQuest is an arcade on steroids. It has all the normal games and stuff, but the main focus is the interactive games. For example, in the Virtual Jungle Cruise you climb onto an actual raft and grab a paddle and start steering through the rapids. On other rides you can enter into a modular spacecraft and go to rescue colonists who are about to get blown up; fly on Aladdin's magic carpet; have a virtual lightsaber fight with comic book bad guys; and be the puck in a hockey-style pinball game.

The star attraction is CyberSpace Mountain. You start with a certain amount of time on the clock and a certain number of feet of track, and Bill Nye the Science Guy helps you design a coaster. You can build in as many flips, spirals, and rolls as you like, program in the speed, and you even get to name the sucker. When you've finished, your coaster is given a scariness rating from 1 to 5, with 1 being sort of a

"Grandma takes a drive in the country" and 5 being pretty much nonstop flips. (If you end up with a coaster too wild or too tame, you can redesign it.)

Then you enter a booth, are strapped into a car, feed the card with your designed coaster into the system, and ride a virtual re-creation of the coaster you just designed, complete with real flips and turns.

Needless to say, it's easy to get hooked on this stuff, going back over and over to design a new coaster, and the line for CyberSpace Mountain is the longest in DisneyQuest, so head there first.

Not all the DisneyQuest attractions are body-slamming. The Animation Academy runs

Insider's Secret

A DISNEYQUEST NAVIGATOR TOLD US THAT MOST PEOPLE START OFF MAKING THEIR COASTERS TOO TAME AND END UP GOING BACK TO BUILD IN MORE SPEED OR FLIPS. HE ADVISES YOU TO START WITH AT LEAST A LEVEL 3 OR 4.

Scare Factor

Most people think designing the coaster at DisneyQuest is a big part of the fun, but if you just want to go for maximum action, ask one of the navigators for their wildest preprogrammed coaster. It has thirteen inversions!

several times a day, and it's a blast because they teach you how to draw a character, or you can design a virtual toy or morph your face.

DisneyQuest is on five different levels, so you can spend a lot of time there. Since a lot of the games have a sort of "team" theme, it's a great place to go with a whole gang of people. The deal is that $26 gets you in, and you play as much as you like for as long as you like.

Helpful Hint

Think a rainy day would be the perfect time to visit DisneyQuest? So do ten zillion other people. The arcade is at its most crowded on rainy days and at night. If you want to try everything, go in the morning.

Cirque du Soleil: Cirque du Soleil is unlike anything you've ever seen before. The show, which is in the white tent-top building near DisneyQuest in the West Side, has amazing acrobats who use these really wild sets and costumes to tell a whole story. Don't expect any elephants or men shot out of cannons; Cirque du Soleil is more like theater than a regular circus, and—although hardly anyone can really describe it—the teens we talked to all thought it was great.

Tickets are $57 (gulp!), so maybe this would be a

"I don't know what I just saw (**Cirque du Soleil**), but I loved it."

Andi, 17

good time to bond with your parents. The show runs twice daily, five days a week. For more information, check out www.cirquedusoleil.com.

SPORTS AT WALT DISNEY WORLD

Disney World has just about every kind of sporting option you can imagine, especially if you're staying at one of the Disney hotels. For general information on sports, call 407-824-2621. They can tell you all about the golf courses, tennis courts, horseback riding, fishing, parasailing, and other things you can sign up for. We've decided just to focus on some of the more popular stuff.

Boat Rental

Several of the Disney resorts have their own boat rentals, but anyone, even those not staying at a Disney hotel, can rent boats at the Downtown Disney Marketplace. You can also take the Magic Kingdom monorail over to any of the hotels on the Seven Seas Lagoon (the Polynesian, Wilderness Lodge, Contemporary, or Grand Floridian) and rent boats there. There's more room to explore if you rent at the Seven Seas Lagoon, so we like it better. (If you're not a guest of the hotel, they'll ask to see a Walt Disney World

Insider's Secret

A GREAT WAY TO BREAK UP A HOT SUMMER DAY AT THE MAGIC KINGDOM IS TO HOP THE MONORAIL OVER TO THE CONTEMPORARY, POLYNESIAN, OR GRAND FLORIDIAN AND RENT A MOUSE BOAT FOR A HALF HOUR. IT'LL COOL YOU OFF FAST, AND THEN YOU CAN GO RIGHT BACK TO THE MAGIC KINGDOM.

ticket and at least one person's—like a parent's—driver's license.)

The most popular type of boat is the Mouse Boat—those zippy little white speedboats you see everywhere. Drivers have to be twelve years old (fourteen at Downtown Disney), and they cost $16 for a half hour. The Mouse Boats hold two people, although, to be honest, you'll go a lot faster if you just have one person per boat. If your whole family wants to be together (we know, gag), you can rent pontoon boats for $33 an hour.

Helpful Hint

If a whole group of you goes out in the Mouse Boats, it can be easy to get separated. Make sure everybody has a waterproof watch and knows what time to get back to the marina. And—we know this tip from experience, right Brennon and Courtney?—write down the numbers of the other boats in your party, so if you lose somebody it's easier for the Disney security people to find them.

Miniature Golf

You're probably thinking, what's so special about miniature golf? But Disney has two themed courses that are definitely different from anything you'll find at the old putt-a-rama back home. Fantasia Gardens, right outside the BoardWalk resort, is the first one . . . and it's got lots of squirting, singing fountains and statues. The course itself is flat hard to play, but at least you have all those cute Fantasia characters around to cheer you on while you're going for putt number nine.

The second course, Winter Summerland, is near Blizzard Beach. The idea is Santa has gone south on vacation, and you can choose to play on either snow or sand—in other words, to play either the summer or winter course. It's kind of a kick to be squirted by snowmen and listening to carols when it's a hundred degrees outside. If you play, bring your camera. There are probably a hundred cute places to take pictures.

It costs $9.25 to play any of the courses, and it gets really crowded at night.

Disney's Wide World of Sports

All kinds of teams (including the Atlanta Braves) use this multimillion-dollar sports complex for training. If you want to see who's playing while you're in town, call Ticketmaster at 407-839-3900.

But the real kick of the Wide World of Sports is the NFL Experience. If you've ever dreamed about firing off a pass like John Elway or saving the game with a field goal in the final seconds, all your football fantasies can come true. An interactive football playground designed like a training camp, the NFL Experience lets you throw in the Quarterback Challenge, catch in Down and Out, and block against the time clock in the Big Move.

We liked Sudden Death, where you try to kick a field goal against a defensive line made out of life-size tackling dummies on a moving track. The losers can buy the winners lunch at the All-Star Café, which is right in the complex. Entrance to the Wide World of Sports is $9 for adults, and the hours for the NFL Experience are 10 A.M. to 5 P.M. Call 407-363-6000 for details.

Universal
Orlando

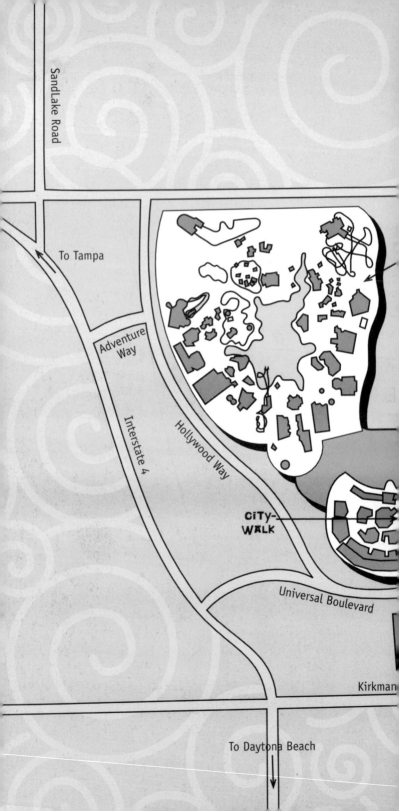

Universal
Orlando

Turkey Lake Road

OS OF
NTURE

UNIVERSAL
STUDIOS
ORLANDO

Vineland Road

HARD ROCK
HOTEL

PORTOFINO
BAY HOTEL

Major Boulevard

PARKING GARAGES

It used to be everybody went to Disney for the week and spent maybe one day at Universal Studios. Not anymore. Universal is really taking aim at Disney by adding high-tech attractions like the new Men in Black ride to Universal, and by opening a dining and entertainment complex, CityWalk, that's a lot like Pleasure Island. But the biggest change is that Universal has opened a whole new theme park, Islands of Adventure, with several teen-oriented attractions.

Insider's Secret

THE MAJOR DiFFERENCE BETWEEN DiSNEY AND UNIVERSAL iS THAT UNIVERSAL'S RiDES ARE MUCH WiLDER AND SCARiER— WHETHER OR NOT THAT'S A GOOD THiNG iS UP TO YOU.

Universal Orlando is what they call the whole complex, which is made up of Universal Studios, Islands of Adventure, and CityWalk. One hotel, Portofino Bay, is already open, and the Hard Rock Hotel is scheduled to open in late 2000. We weren't able to check it out before we went to press, but how can it help but be anything but great?

Now, all of a sudden, Universal Orlando is a major attraction in its own right, taking two or three days to do it right instead of just one. With this in mind, you've got different ticket options (all prices are for adults):

- **One-day, one-park pass: $46**

- **Two-day Orlando Pass: $80**

- **Three-day Orlando Pass: $100**

- **Four-day Orlando Pass: $120**

The one-day pass gets you into *either* Islands of Adventure or Universal Studios, while the multiday passes get you into both parks. And, unlike Disney World, at Universal Orlando things are close together. You can walk from one park to another and stop for lunch at CityWalk along the way.

GETTiNG TO UNiVERSAL ORLANDO

Getting there is pretty simple. If you're staying at a Universal hotel, you take the water taxi. If you're driving, you follow signs from I-4. The parking deck is a long, long way from the parks, but once you're there, everything's connected and it's a breeze.

7

Universal Studios

THE BIG STUFF

All the rides at Universal are based on movies. Major attractions are Men in Black, Back to the Future, Terminator 2: 3D, and Jaws.

UNIVERSAL ATTRACTIONS

Men in Black: Remember the scene in the movie where Will Smith is trying to become a trainee? That's you, and this ride takes the basic idea of Buzz Lightyear in Disney World and turns up the heat about a million degrees.

Insider's Secret

AT MEN IN BLACK, THERE ARE TWELVE DIFFERENT RIDE ENDINGS DEPENDING ON THE COMBINED SCORE TOTALS OF THE PEOPLE IN YOUR VEHICLE. WHICH MEANS YOU CAN RIDE MORE THAN ONCE AND HAVE A DIFFERENT SCORE AND DIFFERENT EXPERIENCE EVERY TIME.

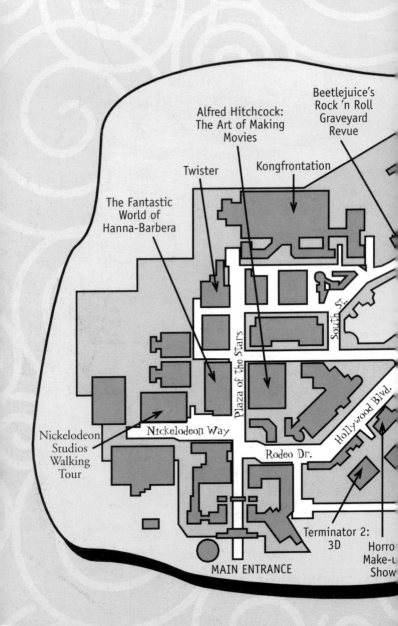

Beetlejuice's Rock 'n Roll Graveyard Revue

Alfred Hitchcock: The Art of Making Movies

Kongfrontation

Twister

The Fantastic World of Hanna-Barbera

South St.

Plaza of the Stars

Hollywood Blvd.

Nickelodeon Studios Walking Tour

Nickelodeon Way

Rodeo Dr.

Terminator 2: 3D

Horro Make-u Show

MAIN ENTRANCE

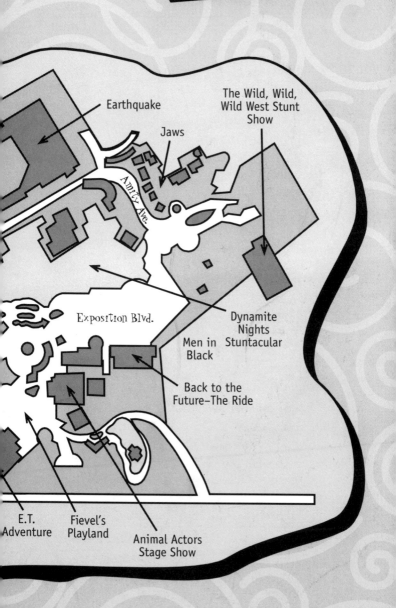

Universal Studios

Earthquake

Jaws

The Wild, Wild, Wild West Stunt Show

Amity Ave.

Exposition Blvd.

Dynamite Nights Stuntacular

Men in Black

Back to the Future–The Ride

E.T. Adventure

Fievel's Playland

Animal Actors Stage Show

Quick Guide to

Attraction	Location
A Day in the Park with Barney	Universal
Alfred Hitchcock: The Art of Making Movies	Universal
The Animal Actors Stage Show	Universal
Back to the Future	Universal
Beetlejuice's Graveyard Revue	Universal
Earthquake	Universal
E.T. Adventure	Universal
Fievel's Playland	Universal
The Funtastic World of Hanna-Barbera	Universal
Men in Black	Universal
The Horror Makeup Show	Universal
Jaws	Universal
Kongfrontation	Universal
The Nickelodeon Tour	Universal
Terminator 2: 3D	Universal
Twister	Universal
The Wild West Stunt Show	Universal
Woody Woodpecker's Kid Zone	Universal

Scare Factor
 ! = Even your grandmother could ride this!
 !! = A couple of **GOTCHA**! moments.
 !!! = Serious thrills here!

Universal Attractions

Speed of Line	Duration of Ride/Show	Scare Factor	Cool Factor
Fast	15 min.	!	✔
Fast	40 min.	!!	✔✔
Fast	20 min.	!	✔✔
Moderate	7 min.	!!!	✔✔✔
Fast	20 min.	!!	✔✔
Moderate	20 min.	!!	✔✔
Slow	5 min.	!	✔✔
Moderate	n/a	!	✔
Moderate	10 min.	!!	✔✔✔
Fast	25 min.	!!!	✔✔✔
Fast	5 min.	!!	✔✔
Moderate	7 min.	!!!	✔✔✔
Fast	10 min.	!!	✔✔
Moderate	30 min.	!	✔
Slow	15 min.	!!!	✔✔
Fast	16 min.	!!	✔✔
Moderate	1 min.	!	✔✔
Moderate	6 min.	!	✔

Cool Factor
   ✔ = Totally lame!
   ✔✔ = Might be fine if you have time.
   ✔✔✔ = Don't miss this ride!

"**Men in Black** is the best ride at Universal, no question."
David, 15

You're riding through the streets of New York, armed with these huge Alienator guns shooting at 120 animatronic aliens. A couple of things make it special. First of all, the aliens not only look real but they shoot back, and if they hit your MIB training vehicle, you go spinning out of control. Second, the score of everybody in your car is combined, so you're not competing with each other, you're playing against another car of tourists that starts at the same time. Depending on how you do, you either end the ride with a hero's welcome in Times Square or by getting kicked out of the MIB program.

Helpful Hint

Whatever is newest is hottest, and Men in Black is Universal's newest ride. Go first thing in the morning if you can.

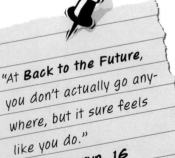

"At **Back to the Future**, you don't actually go anywhere, but it sure feels like you do."
Caryn, 16

Back to the Future: The preshow explains it all. Bad-boy Biff has stolen one of Doc Brown's time machines, and it's up to you to get into one of the Delore-ans and bring him back. It's like a simulated high-speed chase through the prehistoric era, and it's a whole lot rougher than Star Tours or Body Wars at Disney. At one point, a dinosaur swallows you.

Scare Factor

Back to the Future is the wildest ride in the park.

Insider's Secret

IF YOU'RE RIDING IN THE FRONT SEAT OF THE DELOREAN, LOOK AROUND. YOU'LL SEE OTHER CARS ALL AROUND YOU ALSO ALONG FOR THE "RIDE." BACK TO THE FUTURE IS REALLY LIKE THE ULTIMATE DRIVE-IN MOVIE.

Jaws: Remember the movie with the shark that ate everyone? Well, it's back and this time it's after you. You're on a sweet little boat tour of Amity Beach and all of a sudden that "Da-dum" music starts. The shark chases you into a boathouse, across a flaming oil spill, and it pops out really close to the boat a couple of times—but thanks to your guide and a bunch of ammo, you end up making it back to Amity pier in one piece. You'd think after four movies and a ride, people would be getting a clue to get out of that town.

Insider's Secret

IF YOU'RE REALLY BRAVE, RIDE JAWS AT NIGHT. THE "SHARK IN THE DARK" EFFECTS ARE EVEN SCARIER.

FunFactoid

It only cost Steven Spielberg $6 million to make Jaws in the seventies; Universal has spent $50 million on the ride!

Terminator 2: 3D: A real split of opinion on this show. If you liked the *Terminator* movies, you'll be into it. If you didn't, you'll be like, "Exactly what is going on here?"

The show is loud and intense, with a mix of live action and film sequences. Probably the best special effect is when the actors seem to emerge from the movie screen onto the stage and later run back "into" the movie.

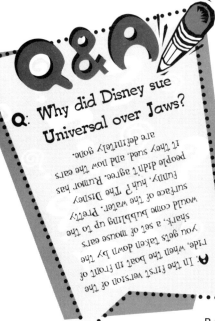

Q: Why did Disney sue Universal over Jaws?

A: In the first version of the ride, when the boat in front of you gets taken down by the shark, a set of mouse ears would come bubbling up to the surface of the water. Pretty funny, huh? The Disney people didn't agree. Rumor has it they sued, and now the ears are definitely gone.

Earthquake: This is both a ride and a show—a show that can star you. They choose extras from the audience to shoot a scene where a department store gets caught in the quake and all these foam rubber bricks start falling. Be sure to volunteer, because it's fun.

Everybody's an extra in the next scene, where a subway station breaks apart and floods. You're loaded into subway cars, and the effects are great—fire from a propane truck on one side, gushing water from broken pipes on the other. Keep your eyes on the set as the ride ends; it's really neat to see how everything that's been knocked over pops back into place and the walls come back together to get ready for the next group.

E.T. Adventure: The movie might have made you cry, but the show lifts you off the ground. You get onto bikes like the ones Eliot rode and fly through the sky,

Insider's Secret

PAY CLOSE ATTENTION TO HOW E.T. TELLS YOU GOOD-BYE AT THE END OF THE RIDE.

over police cars, past the moon, and back to E.T.'s planet. E.T. is in the basket of the middle bike in the front row and he sticks his head up every minute or two.

The Funtastic World of Hanna-Barbera: We know, this sounds like a stupid kiddie ride, but it's not. In the preshow—which is narrated by Hanna and Barbera, the guys who draw the cartoons—you learn that Dick Dastardly has kidnapped Elroy Jetson and it's up to you, along with Yogi Bear and Boo Boo, to rescue him.

Great idea, but there's one problem. Yogi is not much of a pilot, so it turns out to be a really rough ride. Yogi almost runs down the Flintstones, the gang from Scooby Doo, and the rest of the Jetsons along the way. The motion-simulation effects are good, and it's fun to feel like you've entered a cartoon.

Insider's Secret

IF YOU DON'T FEEL LIKE YOU HAVE THE STOMACH FOR THE FUNTASTIC WORLD, OR YOU'VE GOT SIBLINGS TOO SMALL TO RIDE, THERE'S A PLACE IN THE FRONT WHERE YOU CAN SIT AND STILL WATCH THE MOVIE.

Kongfrontation: The idea is that you're in a New York train station and King Kong is on the loose. Do we even have to tell you that he's headed right your way? You come really close to the mega-ape a couple of times, and can even smell his hot banana-breath right in your face. At the end he grabs your tram and "drops" it, although there's not much of a fall; be sure to look at the monitors as you exit. It turns out your close call with death has made the evening news.

Insider's Secret

DO THE RIDES IN THE MORNING, AND SAVE THE SHOWS FOR THE AFTERNOON.

Helpful Hint

As you leave Kongfrontation, you can pose inside of King Kong's hand for a picture. It makes a fun and not-too-expensive souvenir.

Twister: In the preshow, Helen Hunt and Bill Paxton, the stars of the movie, tell you how dangerous tornadoes are. But that's not what you came for. You came to stand in the middle of a five-story-high twister that they make right before your eyes on a soundstage. You've got stuff crashing and

"It really was like being in the middle of the movie (Twister)."

Tyler, 13

swirling all around you, and yeah, the flying cow is back for another lap. The ride is loud, wet, and has a couple of "gotcha" moments that you don't see coming. Just be sure to have a hairbrush for afterward.

Alfred Hitchcock: The Art of Making Movies: You see scenes from scary Hitchcock movies, and the best part is when you put on 3-D glasses and it looks like a bunch of crows from *The Birds* are coming right at you. Then they take you in another room and show you how they shot the shower scene in *Psycho*, using an audience volunteer. Very interesting if you like old horror movies, pretty interesting even if you don't.

The Horror Make-Up Show: This show is about how they use make-up to create special effects in horror movies. That's probably enough right there to tell you if you want to see it.

The Wild West Stunt Show: Don't miss this hysterical show. Some regular stunt guys start out showing you their tricks, then some "bad guys" try to take over the show and it gets really out of hand. It's all total slapstick, silly and wild, with major stunts thrown in so casually that they don't seem as dangerous as they are.

Insider's Secret

WE DON'T WANT TO GIVE ANYTHING AWAY, BUT IF IT'S A HOT DAY, YOU MIGHT WANT TO SIT BY THE WELL (AT THE WILD WEST STUNT SHOW).

The Animal Actors Stage Show: A really cute, funny show, starring all kinds of animals doing their tricks. A lot of the attractions at Universal are either really scary or really babyish, but this is one show everybody in the family will like.

Insider's Secret

ARE YOUR PARENTS PRESSURING YOU TO SPEND TIME WITH THE FAMILY? GOOD ATTRACTIONS FOR EVERYONE, NO MATTER WHAT THEIR AGE, ARE E.T. ADVENTURE, THE FUNTASTIC WORLD OF HANNA-BARBERA, THE WILD WEST STUNT SHOW, AND THE ANIMAL ACTORS STAGE SHOW.

Beetlejuice's Graveyard Revue: A loud, goofy rock-and-roll musical starring all kinds of movie monsters. Not the best show in the park, but it's okay and a good place to rest in the afternoon. You can eat lunch while you watch.

The Kiddie Stuff: The Barney show is for babies and toddlers, and pretty much torture for anyone over four. The Woody Woodpecker Kid Zone is for kids a little bit older, and it's got a small coaster that jerks you around a whole lot more than it looks like it will. Curious George Goes to Town really ought to be called Curious George Goes to the Car Wash—it's this totally wet water play area. Fievel's Playland is a big play area with all sorts of things for kids to climb on, slides, and a really neat little water raft ride. We're telling you this just in case you're in the park with younger siblings or kids you're babysitting, since this is definitely not an area where you see a lot of teens.

Nickelodeon Studios is also at Universal. The tours are for kids who are really into the Game Lab games, getting slimed and junk like that. But sometimes they're taping shows, too, and that can be fun to watch. If a show is taping on the day you visit, you can get tickets as you enter the park. Who knows, your family might get the chance to climb through a bunch of glop for a cheesy first-place prize!

Insider's Secret

ONE OF THE BEST SHOWS AT UNIVERSAL IS A STREET SHOW IN THE NEW YORK SECTION STARRING THE BLUES BROTHERS. CHECK YOUR MAP FOR SHOWTIMES.

PARADES AND SHOWS

Check your map for the time and location of street shows. We like the Blues Brothers the best.

The closing show is called the Dynamite Nights Spectacular, and it's a boat stunt show in the big lagoon. You've got a choice. Since the show is water-level instead of high in the sky like the Disney fireworks, you need to get there early enough to get a good place by the water or else you won't see anything. And by this point in the day, you may have seen plenty of things blow up. (What is it with Universal and fire, anyway?) If you decide to skip the show, this is a good time to go back to any ride you really liked earlier in the day. Lines usually aren't as long right before closing.

WHERE TO EAT

Louie's has good Italian food, Mel's Dine-in has shakes and burgers, and there are plenty of fast places to get a bite. Your best bet is to visit the Hard Rock Café, which has an entrance that goes directly into the restaurant from Universal, located near Nick Studios. Just go either early or late. From noon to 2 P.M., the place is packed.

You could also exit the park and eat in CityWalk. It's not a far walk.

WHERE TO SHOP

Every attraction lets you out through a gift shop that sells souvenirs from the movie that the ride was based on. In other words, you can get *Twister* stuff, *Back to the Future* stuff, *Men in Black* stuff, a stuffed *Jaws* shark . . . all kinds of stuff. It's set up for impulse buying—you know, you're high on the ride you just did, so you buy something you're sick of in five minutes. So we say ride everything, look at all the merchandise, and do your actual shopping at the end of the day.

UNIVERSAL STUDIOS "DON'T MISS" LIST

- ∞ *Men in Black*
- ∞ *Back to the Future*
- ∞ *Jaws*
- ∞ *Twister*
- ∞ *The Animal Actors Stage Show*
- ∞ *The Wild West Stunt Show*
- ∞ *The Funtastic World of Hanna-Barbera*

And, depending on your tastes, you might really like:

- ∞ *Terminator 2: 3D*
- ∞ *Earthquake*
- ∞ *Kongfrontation*
- ∞ *E.T. Adventure*

CHAPTER 8

Islands of Adventure and CityWalk

Universal's newest park, Islands of Adventure, opened in 1999, and it has some major thrills. You enter through Port of Entry, which works sort of like Main Street in the Magic Kingdom, with lots of shops, places to eat, and "business" stuff like lockers and Guest Relations. From there the park is laid out pretty much in a circle, with five individual islands, each with totally different themes.

Helpful Hint

Ride the big deal stuff early in the morning, then do some shows and minor rides in the afternoon. Islands of Adventure is laid out in a way that makes it easy to walk around, so there's no reason not to make two or three laps through the whole park in a day.

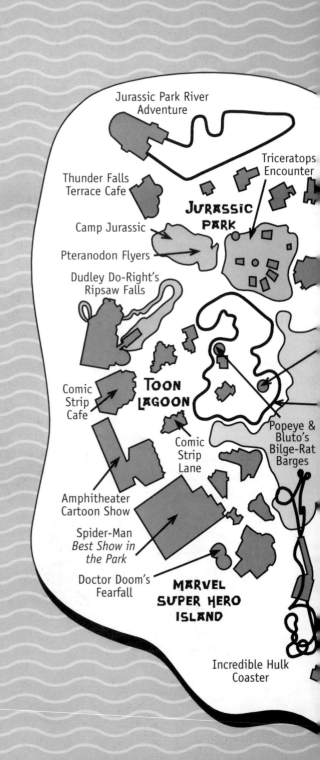

Jurassic Park River
Adventure

Triceratops
Encounter

Thunder Falls
Terrace Cafe

**JURASSIC
PARK**

Camp Jurassic

Pteranodon Flyers

Dudley Do-Right's
Ripsaw Falls

**TOON
LAGOON**

Comic
Strip
Cafe

Popeye &
Bluto's
Bilge-Rat
Barges

Comic
Strip
Lane

Amphitheater
Cartoon Show

Spider-Man
*Best Show in
the Park*

Doctor Doom's
Fearfall

**MARVEL
SUPER HERO
ISLAND**

Incredible Hulk
Coaster

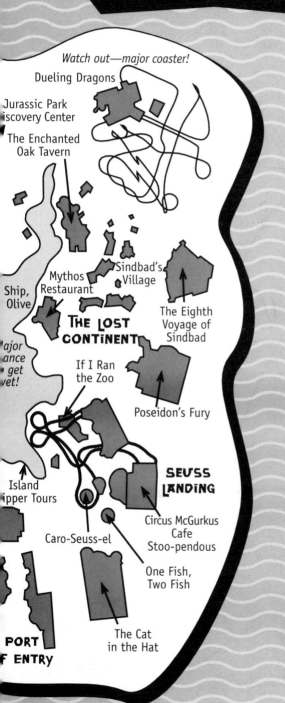

Islands of Adventure

Watch out—major coaster!

Dueling Dragons

Jurassic Park
iscovery Center

The Enchanted
Oak Tavern

Mythos
Restaurant

Sindbad's
Village

Ship,
Olive

**THE LOST
CONTINENT**

The Eighth
Voyage of
Sindbad

ajor
ance
get
vet!

If I Ran
the Zoo

Poseidon's Fury

**SEUSS
LANDING**

Island
ipper Tours

Circus McGurkus
Cafe
Stoo-pendous

Caro-Seuss-el

One Fish,
Two Fish

**PORT
F ENTRY**

The Cat
in the Hat

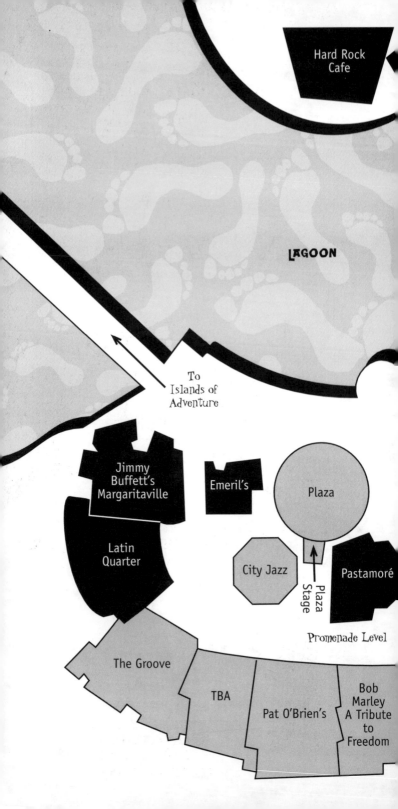

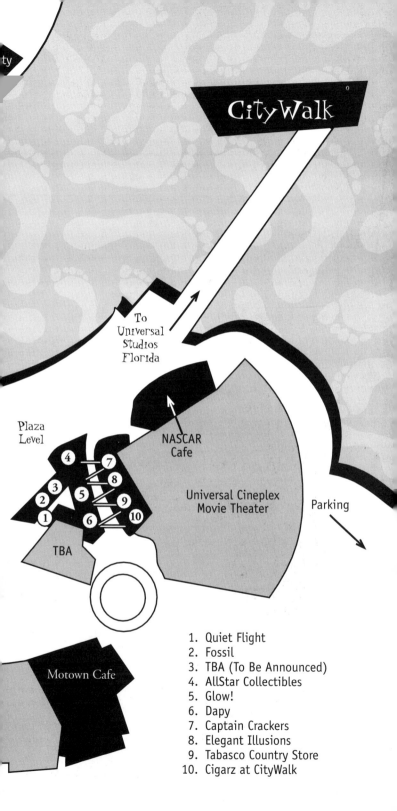

CityWalk

To Universal Studios Florida

Plaza Level

NASCAR Cafe

Universal Cineplex Movie Theater

Parking

TBA

Motown Cafe

1. Quiet Flight
2. Fossil
3. TBA (To Be Announced)
4. AllStar Collectibles
5. Glow!
6. Dapy
7. Captain Crackers
8. Elegant Illusions
9. Tabasco Country Store
10. Cigarz at CityWalk

Quick Guide to

Attraction	Location
Amazing Adventures of Spider-Man	SuperHero Island
Camp Jurassic	Jurassic Park
The Cat in the Hat	Seuss Landing
Caro-Seuss-el	Seuss Landing
Discovery Center	Jurassic Park
Dr. Doom's Fearfall	SuperHero Island
Dudley Do-Right's Ripsaw Falls	Toon Lagoon
Dueling Dragons	Lost Continent
The Eighth Voyage of Sindbad	Lost Continent
If I Ran the Zoo	Seuss Landing
Incredible Hulk Coaster	SuperHero Island
Me Ship, The Olive	Toon Lagoon
One Fish, Two Fish Red Fish, Blue Fish	Seuss Landing
Popeye and Bluto's Bilge-Rat Barges	Toon Lagoon
Poseidon's Fury	Lost Continent
Pteranodon Flyers	Jurassic Park
River Adventure	Jurassic Park
Triceratops Encounter	Jurassic Park

Scare Factor
  ! = Even your grandmother could ride this!
 !! = A couple of **GOTCHA**! moments.
!!! = Serious thrills here!

Islands of Adventure Attractions

Speed of Line	Duration of Ride/Show	Scare Factor	Cool Factor
Moderate	15 min.	!!!	✔✔✔
n/a	n/a	!	✔
Moderate		!	✔✔
Slow	3 min.	!	✔
n/a	n/a	!	✔
Slow	2 min.	!!!	✔✔
Moderate	8 min.	!!	✔✔✔
Moderate	7 min.	!!!	✔✔✔
n/a	25 min.	!!	✔✔
n/a	n/a	!	✔
Moderate	4 min.	!!!	✔✔✔
n/a	n/a	!	✔
Slow	4 min.	!	✔✔
Moderate	12 min.	!!	✔✔✔
n/a	25 min.	!!	✔✔
Slow	6 min.	!	✔
Slow	n/a	!!!	✔✔✔
Slow	20 min.	!	✔

Cool Factor

✔ = Totally lame!

✔✔ = Might be fine if you have time.

✔✔✔ = Don't miss this ride!

Insider's Secret

AS YOU CROSS THE BRIDGE FROM ONE ISLAND TO ANOTHER, PAY ATTENTION TO ALL THE LITTLE THINGS THEY DO TO CHANGE THE MOOD. YOU'LL HEAR WIND CHIMES AS YOU WALK INTO THE LOST CONTINENT, FOR EXAMPLE.

THE BIG STUFF

Spider-Man, the Incredible Hulk Coaster, Dudley Do-Right's Ripsaw Falls, Jurassic Park River Adventure, and Dueling Dragons can all draw major lines late in the day—especially Spider-Man and Dudley Do-Right.

ISLANDS OF ADVENTURE ATTRACTIONS

Marvel Super Hero Island

You're inside a comic book world here, and all three of the rides are total scream-rippers. Turn left as you leave Port of Entry and you'll enter Super Hero Island . . . it's the right way to start the day.

Spider-Man: Probably the most entertaining ride in Universal Escape, Spider-Man has it all: 3-D effects and motion-simulation combined with an actual moving ride. The deal: All the villains from the *Spider-Man*

"You'll probably—no, you'll definitely want to ride **Spider-Man** more than once, so be sure to hit it early when there's no lines."
Kyle, 15

"**Spider-Man** is the best ride of the whole trip."
Max, 16

comics have joined forces to steal the Statue of Liberty and take over New York City. (Where else? Why do the bad guys never hit Tulsa or Baltimore?) Spider-Man, the newspaper reporter/super hero, has disappeared and the newspaper chief is so desperate that he's ready to send a bunch of tourists (you) out in the Scoopmobile to get the story.

The villains throw everything they've got at you; you're shocked, spun, splashed, misted, and finally "dropped" from the top of a 400-foot building. It's a simulated drop, of course, but it feels really real and is one of the best effects of any ride in Orlando. Which makes it one of the best effects in the world. Does Spider-Man show up just in time to save you? Hey, is this your first time on a theme park ride, or what?

Helpful Hint

For the wildest ride, sit in the back row of the Scoopmobile. For the best 3-D effects, sit in the front. For a little bit of both, sit in the middle.

Insider's Secret

AT SPIDER-MAN, BE SURE TO LISTEN TO THE PRESHOW FILMS AS YOU GO THROUGH THE LINE. THEY NOT ONLY SET UP THE STORY, BUT THEY'RE HILARIOUS, ESPECIALLY THE INSTRUCTIONAL VIDEO ON HOW TO LOAD THE SCOOPMOBILE.

Dr. Doom's Fearfall: The two tall towers you see as you approach Super Hero Island are this ride. The story is that Dr. Doom has invented a machine that can suck the fear out of you, and he wants to use these big pots of fear to take over the world. The ride shoots you 180 feet in the air—the first lift is definitely the wildest part. From there you plunge, dangle, rise, and fall again. Some people are a little freaked out by the fact that there's nothing under their feet; you really do feel like you're hanging.

"If you can survive the first five seconds of Dr. Doom's Fearfall, you'll be fine."
Amanda, 15

Incredible Hulk Coaster: This is a major, major coaster that makes seven inversions and reaches speeds of 40 mph. It starts with a total bang—a "cannon shot" beginning that propels you into your first flip. Most of the ride takes place over water, and at a couple of points you go plunging underground into tunnels filled with fog. Although the ride is wild, it's very smooth, and some people who don't like to be jerked around on coasters love the Hulk for just that reason.

"When you come out of the first flip at **Incredible Hulk**, you feel completely weightless for about three seconds."

Franco, 16

Scare Factor

If you want to see what's coming on the **Incredible Hulk Coaster**, get in the separate line for people who want the front row.

Toon Lagoon

Can you spell water, boys and girls? Toon Lagoon is also a cartoon world, but this one is home to the more happy, funny, kiddielike comics. There's a cartoon show for the kids, or they can play on Popeye's boat, called "Me Ship, the Olive." But the big attractions are two water rides.

Dudley Do-Right's Ripsaw Falls: The last drop here is seventy-five feet— to give you

"I loved **Ripsaw Falls**, but I've got to warn you . . . wrap your plastic poncho thing around your butt because water gets all the way in the log, and if you aren't careful, you'll end up with a dry top and a wet bottom."

Andrea, 13

some idea what that means, Splash Mountain drops fifty-two feet. It looks like you're falling into a shack full of TNT, so there's an explosion effect, too, and so much water flies up that you'll get soaking wet. The whole ride is very fun, very cute, and it includes all the Dudley characters, from mean old Snively to loyal Horse to "I got no luck at all" heroine Nell. And it's very wet—did we mention that?

Helpful Hint

Dudley Do-Right's Ripsaw Falls draws long lines, mostly because it takes so much time to load people into the logs. Usually when a ride is popular, we tell you to ride it first thing in the morning or at night, since that is when the crowd isn't as bad . . . but you might not want to be dripping wet at 8 A.M. Or 10 P.M. Our advice? Either cover up with a rain poncho and ride in the morning and night or come in the afternoon when it's hot and realize you'll probably ride it just once.

Popeye and Bluto's Bilge-Rat Barges: This is a really, really wild whitewater ride for the whole family. You climb into these circular boats, but the big difference between this ride and Kali River Rapids at Disney's Animal Kingdom is that here *everybody* gets wet. Even if you managed to get through the ride without a huge splash, you'll get caught in Sweet

"Bilge-Rat Barges is the ultimate when it comes to water. . . . Between the waterfalls, the dips, those people on the Miss Olive squirting at you, and the boat wash, you will not leave this ride dry."

Leigh, 15

Helpful Hint

Take off your shoes, socks, and your watch, and if you're wearing pants, roll them up. You might be laughing now, but trust us, when you join all the people standing on the dock after they ride Bilge-Rat Barges trying to wring water out their clothes, you won't be.

Pea's Boat Wash at the end. Just make sure you go at a time when you want to cool off.

Jurassic Park

This part of the park looks just like the movie! You might get chills when you walk through the big stone gates and on the other side hear the dinos rambling around in the bushes and see their footprints on the concrete walkway.

River Adventure: You're supposed to be taking a nice little tour of the innocent plant-eating dinos and—We know you won't believe this—something goes wrong. Your boat goes off course into a raptor containment area, where those nasty little guys have taken over the system and let all the dinos loose. Finally, you're chased down a hill by a T-Rex and the drop is eighty-five feet, which makes both Splash Mountain and Dudley Do-Right look like kiddie rides.

But the drop doesn't feel quite that wild for two reasons. One, you start the fall inside a building and

Helpful Hint

At River Adventure, only the people in the front and the sides get too wet. And your picture is being taken on the way down, so smile!

end it outside the building, so you can't see where you're going. Two, it's a huge boat—five seats in five rows. But it still gives you that kicked-in-the-stomach feeling.

Triceratops Encounter: This isn't a ride or a show, just the chance to view an audio-animatronic dinosaur who can blink, sneeze, move, and even pee. You pretty much stand around and look at her while a guy talks like she's a real dino, so if you want to get more into the action, volunteer to be one of the people who goes up to touch her. That's kind of creepy in a neat way . . . she feels real. Or at least the way you'd imagine a dinosaur would feel.

Pteranodon Flyers: There's a big children's play area called Camp Jurassic, and it has a neat little aerial ride, Pteranodon Flyers, where you can float over the park. There's a reverse height requirement, though, so you can only ride if you're with a kid. And the line gets longer than Dudley Do-Right, so only try it if you've got lots of time.

Discovery Center: Remember the welcome center in Jurassic Park? This one looks just like it. It's right across the lagoon from where you enter the park in the morning, so when you get to the end of Port of Entry, stop for a second and look across the water. It's great.

Inside the center is a big interactive area where you can watch a baby raptor hatch from an egg or play dino trivia. Lots of the exhibits are for little kids, but it's fun to stop in for a minute or two.

The Lost Continent

This is a misty, mysterious island, with one of Island of Adventure's wildest attractions, Dueling Dragons.

Dueling Dragons: Like the name suggests, this is really two coasters in one: the "fire" dragon and the "ice" dragon fight each other during the ride, and on three different times they come so close to each other (within twelve inches!) that it looks like you're going to crash.

Dueling Dragons is a suspension-style coaster, which means you hang beneath the track, and there are some major flips and turns. Along with the Hulk, it's the scariest ride in the park.

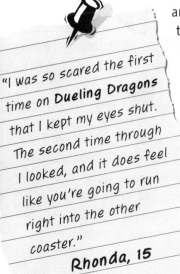

"I was so scared the first time on **Dueling Dragons** that I kept my eyes shut. The second time through I looked, and it does feel like you're going to run right into the other coaster."

Rhonda, 15

Insider's Secret

THE TWO COASTERS TAKE DIFFERENT PATHS. IF YOU RIDE TWICE, BE SURE TO DO ICE ONE TIME, FIRE THE NEXT. THE FIRE COASTER IS FASTER BUT THE ICE COASTER HAS MORE SIDE TO SIDE MOVEMENT.

Scare Factor

At **Dueling Dragons**, if you really want to feel how close you come to the other coaster in the near misses, ask for an outside seat.

The Eighth Voyage of Sindbad: This is Island of Adventure's stunt show. The story is pretty corny compared to Indiana Jones at MGM, but there are some good tricks, especially at the end when the witch character is caught on fire.

Poseidon's Fury: You and about fifty other people are sent into this dark room where a crazy old man starts telling you how the brothers Poseidon and Zeus, two Greek gods, are fighting each other. You walk through a spiraling tunnel of water—which is a really unusual effect—to the sunken city of Atlantis while the crazy old man keeps being, well, crazy. The show ends with a battle between Poseidon and Zeus, which is like a battle between fire and water.

You walk from room to room during this show, which means a new group starts every five minutes, and there's never a very long wait.

Seuss Landing

Seuss Landing is total eye candy, with the colors and shapes right out of a Dr. Seuss book. It's the kiddie section, but you might want to stop and look at the Caro-Seuss-el, where you ride the characters from the Seuss books, or walk through If I Ran the Zoo, a kind of wacky play area. But the rides below are actually fun for any age.

One Fish, Two Fish, Red Fish, Blue Fish: On One Fish, Two Fish you can control how high your fish flies. You're supposed to "follow the book," which is being read to you by this really energetic lady, who says things like, "Red fish fly high, Blue fish go low." Supposedly if you follow the directions, you won't get squirted by the bad fish who are in a circle along the sides of the ride. At one point, you fly on your own and the fish kind of squirt at random. It's silly, but fun.

The Cat in the Hat: We love Disney, but the kiddie rides at Island of Adventure are so, so, so much cooler than those in the Magic Kingdom. Here, you ride through scenes from the Cat in the Hat book on couches, and there's lots of neat effects, as well as some wild spinning when Thing 1 and Thing 2 take over the house and make a major mess. The poor goldfish keeps trying to clean it all up before the mom gets back.

WHERE TO EAT

There are plenty of fast-food places scattered all through Universal, so you never have to wait very long for a meal. Our main advice is to steer clear from Green Eggs and Ham. The green is from parsley . . . but it's still a major yuck.

If you want some entertainment along with your meal, exit the park and eat at CityWalk. It's close, and you have your choice of places, like the Motown Café, Nascar Café, Hard Rock Café, and Jimmy Buffet's Margaritaville.

WHERE TO SHOP

Every section has its own shops tied to the theme of that particular island. The Islands of Adventure Trading Company in Port of Entry is the biggest store, with souvenirs from every section of the park. We like the Mulberry Street Store in Seuss Landing, which has great Grinch Christmas ornaments. There's also some interesting stuff at Shop of Wonders, this sort of tent bazaar section of the Lost Continent. You can even get your palm read there. If you're into trading cards, the Comic Shop on Super Hero Island is the perfect place.

ISLANDS OF ADVENTURE "DON'T MISS" LIST

≋ *Spider-Man*

≋ *Incredible Hulk Coaster*

≋ *Dudley Do-Right's Ripsaw Falls*

≋ *Popeye and Bluto's Bilge-Rat Barges*

≋ *Jurassic Park River Adventure*

≋ *Dueling Dragons*

And you might also enjoy . . .

≋ *One Fish, Two Fish, Red Fish, Blue Fish*

≋ *The Cat in the Hat*

≋ *Poseidon's Fury*

≋ *Doctor Doom's Fearfall*

CITYWALK

CityWalk is the dining, shopping, and entertainment complex that links Islands of Adventure with Universal Studios. CityWalk gives guests at both of the Universal Escape theme parks lots more places to eat.

Just have your hand stamped, exit the park, and head for lunch or dinner at CityWalk.

There are tons of restaurants here, but some of the more casual and fun choices include NBA City, where you can compare your palmprint to that of Patrick Ewing and other basketball stars. Or try the good ol' boy food of Nascar Café, where you dine in cars, the waitstaff dresses like your pit crew, and the utensils look like tools. The Motown Café is great if you're into oldies music, especially when the house band comes out to sing Supremes and Temptation hits. Jimmy Buffet's Margaritaville, where taped Buffet concerts play on screens overhead between live musical acts, is the perfect choice if you're into the Parrothead thing, and of course it serves Cheeseburgers in Paradise. The Latin Quarter is definitely the place if you like spicy food and salsa dancing.

The largest Hard Rock Café in the world is at CityWalk. (Be sure to look up at the electronic marquee, which reads things like, "Green hair, tattoos, and nose rings . . . and that's just the waitress.") Beside the café is the Hard Rock Live auditorium, where both local and nationally known music acts perform. To get a schedule of who is appearing at the clubs, either call 407-224-2189 or go on-line at www.uescape.com.

Food, shopping, and music aside, there's lots in CityWalk to keep you entertained, and it's a great place to hang out after the parks close. (Although after 9 P.M., most of the clubs are closed to teenagers.) On weekend nights there are special performers like extreme sport athletes, who do their stuff on skateboards, bikes, or jet-skis. There's some pretty strange street entertainment, as well as a twenty-screen Cineplex showing the latest movies.

CHAPTER 9

Beyond Disney World: Sea World and Other Orlando Attractions

SEA WORLD

If you've done Disney and you like killer whales and other ocean creatures, spend a day at Sea World. It's actually got some pretty cool stuff—beyond just Shamu!

A day at Sea World costs $46.00 for adults, $37.00 for kids 3 to 9, but you can find discount coupons all over Orlando, or use the Flexticket plan. The park opens at 9 A.M. and you can see everything in a day. Call 407-351-3600 for more information or go to www.shamu.com.

Insider's Secret

SEA WORLD IS LAID OUT SO THAT THE CROWDS PRETTY MUCH FLOW FROM ONE SHOW TO THE NEXT. IF YOU FOLLOW THE SHOW SCHEDULE IN YOUR MAP, YOU'LL SEE ALL THE MAIN STUFF WITHOUT A LOT OF BACKTRACKING.

Kraken

Hold on! Kraken is the hottest new ride at Sea World and it smashes all Orlando records for categories of roller coasters. Count 'em: Tallest. Fastest. Longest. Wildest. Named after a legendary sea monster, this incredibly wicked serpent coaster corkscrews you through the ride of your life. Kraken suspends you in mid-air as high as a 15-story building and turns you head over heels at 65 mph. It's completely crazy!

Scare Factor

Kraken is the scariest ride you'll ever go on! You have no one to hold on to, nothing in front of you, nothing below you—it's floorless!

Journey to Atlantis

This is the ultimate high-speed water ride and coaster rolled into one. The ride designers call it a water coaster, but whatever it's called, you'll want to do it more than once.

To get back to the lost city of Atlantis, the tiny Greek fishing boats twist and dive through the water faster than you'd ever dare drive your car!

Helpful Hint

Okay, time to get out that change of clothes. You'll get soaked on Journey to Atlantis. Not splashed. Soaked!

Scare Factor

You'll see the first drop on Atlantis, which comes out the front of the building, but hold on for the next surprise—a wicked 60-foot S-shaped drop!

Shows

Sea World's main claim to fame is its shows—especially the ones that feature the dolphins, the sea lions and otters, and of course, Shamu. Don't worry—these shows are not just boring oceanography classes. They're pretty fun and interesting, and you should definitely see them. You sit in huge open-air theaters, but if you want a good seat,

"The mime at the Sea Lion preshow is amazing!"
—Bailey, 15

Q&A

Q: What's a group of 10-50 female seals belonging to one male seal called?

A: A harem.

plan to get there about 15 minutes early.

If you're wiped out or your feet are killing you from walking all day, go see the waterskiing show, the acrobatics show, or one of the movies. There's also a few musicals, a Polynesian revue, and a laser light show. If you're really into animals, Pets on Stage features some

Insider's Secret

IF YOU DECIDE TO SIT IN THE "SPLASH ZONE"—THE FIRST 10 ROWS OF THE STADIUM—SHAMU'S GOOD-BYE WAVE WILL LEAVE YOU DRENCHED STRAIGHT THROUGH TO YOUR UNDERWEAR. THAT'S GREAT ON A HOT DAY, BUT IF YOU GO AT NIGHT, BE PREPARED TO FREEZE YOUR BUTT OFF AFTERWARDS.

pretty funny dogs, cats, potbelly pigs, and other animals that were rescued from animal shelters.

Standing Exhibits
Blame it on Mary Poppins or something, but penguins always seem to get you laughing. Sea World

FunFactoid

The whale shark is the world's biggest fish, weighing in at about 15 tons—which is more than two African elephants put together!

has lots of exhibits, and one favorite is the Penguin Encounter, where you can watch these tuxedoed creatures both above and below the ice. Check your entertainment schedule for feeding times, when the trainers slip around on the iceberg with buckets of fish and the penguins waddle determinedly behind them. It's a riot.

"I don't get how the penguins can swallow a whole fish in one gulp!"

—Glenn, 13

Insider's Secret

FOR AN UP-CLOSE-AND-PERSONAL VIEW, CHECK OUT THE **TERRORS OF THE DEEP** EXHIBIT. THE SHARKS AREN'T AS BIG AS "JAWS" BUT THEIR TEETH ARE JUST AS SHARP. IT'S AS CLOSE TO MORAY EELS AND BARRACUDAS AS YOU'LL EVER WANT TO BE.

The California sea lions are at the Pacific Point Preserve. In Key West at Sea World, you'll see Florida's own endangered species, the manatee, along with sea turtles, dolphins, and stingrays. There are also underwater viewing tanks where you can see the animals up close. These are continuous-viewing exhibits that are open all the time.

At Wild Arctic, an exhibit dedicated to Polar Bears, you can get to the top of the exhibit to view the bears either on a motion-simulation helicopter "ride" or by walking.

Q&A

Q: How did the shark get its name?

A: It's from a Latin word that means "sharp teeth." Duh.

FunFactoid

The shock from an electric eel is so strong it can throw someone across a room.

Insider's Secret

THE LINES AT WILD ARCTIC ARE THE LONGEST JUST AFTER THE NEARBY SHAMU SHOW LETS OUT. IF YOU GO WHILE ONE OF THE SHAMU SHOWS IS ON, YOU'LL GET THROUGH MUCH FASTER.

Helpful Hint

For $3 you can get three small fish and toss them to the barking seals, sea lions, or the dolphins. The dolphins and stingrays are in shallow tanks, so be sure to reach over and touch them as they glide by. Slick and slippery!

Educational Tours

If you have to turn in some kind of report when you get back to school, you might want to check out Sea World's educational tours. (Hey, then you'll know the difference between a sea lion and a seal!) They have tours that focus on sharks, polar bears, and Sea World's animal rescue and rehabilitation programs. They're pretty cheap (adults $7, children $6), and reservations aren't necessary; either buy your tour ticket when you purchase your general-admission ticket or return to Guest Relations near the main entrance to get them once inside the park.

"The helicopter ride at **Wild Arctic** isn't quite as crazy as the motion-simulation rides at Disney and Universal."
—**Chandler, 16**

FunFactoid

If a starfish loses one of its arms, that piece will grow into a whole new starfish!

Helpful Hint

If you like this kind of thing, the Dolphin Interaction Program is pretty exciting. You get to put on wet suits and go into the main pool at the Whale and Dolphin Stadium, where you can actually play with the animals while the trainers watch and instruct you. The cost is $159, and you can get more information by calling 407-370-1385.

Camp Sea World

In case you're really getting into this stuff, you or your parents can call for the Camp Sea World brochure at least two months in advance of your trip (800-406-2244 or 407-363-2380). There are one-day classes geared for kids up to eighth-grade as well as five-day classes for more in-depth study of marine animals.

Helpful Hint

Camp Sea World offers over 200 summer camp classes including sleepover programs and courses for families. These activities are popular, so call way ahead. The brochure tells you everything you need to know for any age-group and gets you so fired up that you want to register for everything.

DISCOVERY COVE

Discovery Cove is a new theme park that opened next to Sea World in 2000. It's the only park that lets you have really up-close encounters with dolphins and other sea life. You can actually swim and play with bottlenose dolphins, then snorkel through clouds of fish in a coral reef lagoon. Or just kick back in a hammock for a few hours and soak up some sun.

Helpful Hint

The most unique thing about Discovery Cove is what it doesn't have. Crowds. This is a reservation-only park that admits a limited number of people per day. (1000, to be exact, but everyone is so spread out that it seems like you have a private beach.)

With such a low number of guests, you get lots of one-on-one with the staff, which includes expert trainers (many of them drafted from Sea World, Discovery Cove's sister park).

This place has class! You check in at a concierge desk (!) and from there a guide takes you on a walking tour of the park, explaining all the activities. A swim in the dolphin lagoon is the best part of the day, and the trainers teach you all about dolphin behaviors. You can swim among fish in the coral reef, and get within inches of barracuda and sharks. Don't worry, they're housed behind plexiglass!

Follow the tropical river through the park and you'll pass a cool fishing village and

Q&A

Q: How does a dolphin hear?

A: The dolphin has a small ear opening behind its eyes, but most hearing takes place through its lower jaw.

Insider's Secret

IN THE RAY LAGOON YOU CAN PLAY WITH THE FIERCE LOOKING (BUT ACTUALLY GENTLE) RAYS, WHICH GROW UP TO 4 FEET IN DIAMETER.

an underwater cave. If you go beneath the waterfall you'll end up inside a huge aviary which houses 300 colorful birds from all over the world. In these surroundings, you'll forget you're even in Orlando.

So what's the price for this awesome adventure? $179 per person plus tax. Now, hang on, that price covers beach umbrellas, lounges, towels, lockers, swim and snorkel gear, and lunch (served either in a restaurant or on the beach). Just convince your parents you're really going to learn something here! Certain packages include admission to Sea World next door. For details and reservations (remember, you need

"*Discovery Cove* is a bit pricey but it's worth every penny!"

—Taka, 17

FunFactoid

Some birds will fly upside down to attract a mate.

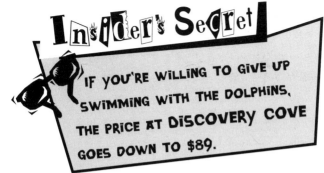

Insider's Secret

IF YOU'RE WILLING TO GIVE UP SWIMMING WITH THE DOLPHINS, THE PRICE AT DISCOVERY COVE GOES DOWN TO $89.

them) call 1-877-4-DISCOVERY. You can also get information on the Internet at www.discoverycove.com.

GATORLAND

This is mostly for younger kids, but if you go, check out the Gator Jumparoo, where the huge gators jump up to five feet out of the water to retrieve chickens from the hands of their trainers. If you like these scaly beasts, you might want to see the Gator Wrestlin' Show, Jungle Crocs of the World, and Snakes of Florida too.

You enter this little place through a giant blue gator mouth and inside, you can get your picture taken holding either an alligator or a boa constrictor. You can also buy a few cans of Gator Chowder at the gift shop—give it to your science teacher back home and maybe he'll raise your grade. And . . . maybe not.

Gatorland admission is $15.97 for adults, $6.94 for kids 3 to 12. Call 800-393-JAWS or 407-855-5496.

FunFactoid

An amazing thing about snakes is that they swallow their meals whole. You're not going to believe this, but some large snakes can swallow whole pigs and sometimes even whole goats. Seriously!

Helpful Hint

Even though Wet 'n Wild is the oldest
water park in Orlando, most kids
we talked to still think it's the best.

WET 'N WILD

If you need to cool off from the Disney rat race, drive
over to Wet 'n Wild. It doesn't have all the atmosphere of River Country or Typhoon Lagoon, but for
sheer thrills, this is the place. Don't forget sun block
and a towel.

Insider's Secret

VISITING THE WATER PARKS
AT NIGHT IS A GREAT IDEA:
LOWER PRICES, SHORTER
LINES, AND YOU DON'T NEED
SUNSCREEN.

The Fuji
Flyer toboggan
ride, the twist-
ing tubes of the
Mach 5, and
the spiraling de-
scent through
the Black Hole
are definitely not
for wimps. Wet
'n Wild's big-deal
attraction, the Bomb Bay, sends
you on a six-second free fall down a 76-foot slide and
is strictly off limits to anyone under 48 inches. These
rides are awesome but can knock the breath out of even
a strong swimmer, so don't
even bother if you're the
chicken-of-the-sea type.

Admission is $28.95
for adults, $22.95 for kids
3 to 9. Discounts—which
often cut admission
price in half— take ef-

"On **Bomb Bay**, my stom
ach was literally in my
mouth!"

—Ian, 16

fect at 3 P.M. during the off-season and at 5 P.M. in summer, when the park stays open until 11 P.M. It's not as crowded at night and besides, there's live entertainment, poolside karaoke, and more of a party atmosphere at night. Think about using the Flexticket, which lets you take in Universal Orlando, Sea World, and Wet 'n Wild. Wet 'n Wild is located on International Drive, which is Exit 30A off I-4. Call 800-992-WILD or 407-351-WILD for details.

MYSTERY FUN HOUSE

This place is full of crazy mazes, sloping floors, and optical illusions and is good for a rainy day. It also has a Jurassic Park miniature golf course and a pretty cool arcade. Admission for all ages is $11. Miniature golf is $10.85.

OFF-SITE DINNER SHOWS (WITH OR WITHOUT THE WHOLE FAM)

Disney isn't the only place in Orlando that has family dinner theaters. You don't go to these places for the food as much as for what goes on while you eat. They cost around $36 for adults and $23 for kids 3 to 11, but look for those discount coupons (some save

Insider's Secret

SOME OF THESE THEATERS ARE GEARED MORE FOR LITTLE KIDS. THE ONES WE LIKED BEST WERE CAPONE'S AND SLEUTH'S MYSTERY DINNER SHOW.

you as much as $10 per dinner) at Guest Services booths or in those freebie magazines you find in hotels and stores. There's usually only one seating per night in the off-season and two during the on-season, so you need to call for exact show times and to make reservations. The halls hold between 400 and 1,000 people and you sit with total strangers at the same table, which *occasionally* can be fun.

Arabian Nights

If you like horses, you'll see more than 60 here, including white Lipizzans and a "mystical unicorn." The best part is the high-speed chariot race re-created from the movie *Ben Hur*. Main course is prime rib. Call 800-553-6116 or 407-396-1787.

FunFactoid

Jesse James and his gang were accredited with at least 10 bank robberies, 7 train robberies, and 4 stagecoach robberies, which added up to over a quarter-million dollars stolen.

Wild Bill's Wild West Show

This show offers knife throwers, rain dancers, lasso twirlers, and a bunch of corny soldiers. Barbecue, fried chicken, and corn on the cob are served up chuck-wagon style. Call 800-883-8181 or 407-351-5151.

Medieval Times

Everyone's divided into competing teams with different colors so you can cheer for "your" knight while you watch him joust on horseback in a

"The best part about Medieval Times is that you get to eat with your fingers. No forks, no knives, no spoons. No kidding."

—Celeste, 17

huge pit. Dinner is roast chicken and ribs. Call 800-229-8300 or 407-239-0214.

King Henry's Feast

This one's a little quieter than Medieval Times. You watch King Henry search for his seventh wife—portraits of her six unlucky predecessors hang in the entry hall—as magicians, jugglers, and minstrels entertain you. Again, chicken and ribs. Call 800-883-8181 or 407-351-5151.

Pirates Adventure

This one is kind of interesting—it's an old B movie that suddenly comes to life on a set of a huge pirate ship surrounded by water. The pirates perform lots of swashbuckling stunts, and everyone in the audience is color-coded to cheer for "their" pirate when the competition starts. The main course is skewered meatballs and chicken—probably to remind you of the losers in the sword fights! Call 407-248-0590.

Capone's

Lots of Italian food to go along with the gangster theme at this place. It's a take-off on a Chicago prohibition-era speakeasy, only done as a musical comedy. Pretty funny stuff, and more pasta than you've seen in your entire life! Call 407-397-2378.

Q: What was Al Capone's real name?

A: Alphonse Capone, born 1899.

Sleuth's Mystery Dinner Show

As you snack on munchies and hang out with the weird characters in this old English drawing room, try not to get sucked in. A crime is about to happen, and it's up to you to question the suspects, add up all the clues, and figure the whole thing out. The group that comes up with the most accurate solution wins a prize. Call 407-363-1985.

Index

A

The ABC Sound Studio, Disney-MGM Studios, 58–59
Adventureland, Magic Kingdom, 30–31
Adventurer's Club, Pleasure Island, 98
Aerosmith, 61–62
Aguilera, Christina, 67
Alfred Hitchcock: The Art of Making Movies, Universal Studios
  description of, 122
  quick guide to, 114–115
All-Star Café, Disney's Wide World of Sports, 104
The Amazing Adventures of Spider-Man, Islands of Adventure
  description of, 134–135
  quick guide to, 132–133
The Animal Actors Stage Show, Universal Studios
  description of, 123
  quick guide to, 114–115
Animal Kingdom. *See also* specific attractions
  big stuff at, 74
  description of attractions, 75–84
  Disney Made Wild, 13
  don't miss list, 85
  eating at, 84
  FASTPASS at, 74
  getting to, 71
  map of, 72–73
  Park Hopper passes for, 7
  photo ops, 79
  quick guide to attractions, 74–75
  school projects at, 10
  shopping in, 84
Animation Academy, Disney-Quest, 101
Animation Magic, Disney Institute, 12
Animation Tour, Disney-MGM Studios, 65
Arabian Nights dinner show, 158
Astro Orbiter, Magic Kingdom
  description of, 30
  quick guide to, 24–25
Atlanta Braves, 104

B

The Backlot Express, Disney-MGM Studios, 69
The Backstage Pass, Disney-MGM Studios
  quick guide to, 58–59
Back to the Future, Universal Studios
  description of, 116–117
  quick guide to, 114–115
Bathing suits, 13
Beach towels, 14

Beastly Bazaar, Animal Kingdom, 84

Beauty and the Beast Stage Show, Disney-MGM Studios
description of, 63
quick guide to, 58–59

Beetlejuice's Graveyard Revue, Universal Studios
description of, 123
quick guide to, 114–115

Behind-the-scenes tours, 13

Big Thunder Mountain Railroad, Magic Kingdom
description of, 33
quick guide to, 24–25

Biology projects, 10

Black Hole, Wet 'n' Wild, 158

Blizzard Beach
after Animal Kingdom, 85
attractions, list of, 90–93
getting to, 87

Blues Brothers Show, Universal Studios, 124

Boardwalk
boat service from, 18
Disney-MGM Studios, getting to, 55
Epcot, getting to, 39

Boats, 18
Mouse Boats, 103
rental boats, 102–103

Body Wars, Epcot
description of, 48–49
quick guide to, 42–43

Bomb Bay, Wet 'n' Wild, 158

Buses, 18

Buzz Lightyear's Space Ranger Spin, Magic Kingdom
description of, 28–29
FASTPASS at, 15
quick guide to, 24–25

C

Cameras and film, 14

Camp Jurassic, Islands of Adventure, 132–133

Camp Sea World, 154

Canada Pavilion, Epcot, 52

Capone's dinner show, 161

Carey, Drew, 64

Caro-Seuss-el, Islands of Adventure, 132–133

Carousel of Progress, Magic Kingdom, 30
quick guide to, 24–25

Car transportation, 19–20

Castaway Creek, Typhoon Lagoon, 95

The Cat in the Hat, Islands of Adventure, 143

China Pavilion, Epcot, 51

Christmas holiday, 3

Cinderella's Castle, Magic Kingdom
eating at, 36
Tinkerbell's Flight, 36

Cinderella's Golden Carrousel, Magic Kingdom, 24–25

Circle of Life, Epcot, 42–43

Cirque du Soleil, DisneyQuest, 99, 101–102

CityWalk, 108, 144–145
map of, 130–131
restaurants at, 145

Comic Shop, Islands of Adventure, 143

Conservation Station, Animal Kingdom, 10

Contemporary
boat rentals at, 102
boat service from, 18
Epcot, getting to, 39
Magic Kingdom, getting to, 21
monorail routes, 16–17

Coral Reef Restaurant, Epcot, 52

Cosmic Ray's Starlight Café, Magic Kingdom, 36

Countdown to Extinction, Animal Kingdom, xiv
description of, 79–80

FASTPASS at, 16
quick guide to, 74–75
Country Bear Jamboree, Magic
Kingdom, 33
quick guide to, 24–25
Cranium Command, Epcot
description of, 49
quick guide to, 42–43
Cretaceous Trail, Animal King-
dom, 10
Cronkite, Walter, 65
Cross Country Creek, Blizzard
Beach, 93
Curtis, Jamie Lee, 45
CyberSpace Mountain, Disney-
Quest, 99–102

D

A Day in the Park with Barney,
Universal Studios
description of, 123
quick guide to, 114–115
December visits, 6
DeGeneres, Ellen, 45
Diamond Horseshoe Jamboree,
Magic Kingdom, 33
Dinner shows, off-site, 159–162
Discovery Center, Islands of
Adventure
description of, 140
quick guide to, 132–133
Discovery Cove,
description, 154–157
pricing, 156
Disney Institute, 11–13
adult classes at, 13
Disney Made Wild, Disney Institute, 13
Disney-MGM Studios. *See also*
specific attractions
description of attractions,
60–67
don't miss list, 70
eating at, 69
getting to, 55
map of, 56–57

parades at, 68
Park Hopper passes for, 7
quick guide to, 58–59
shopping at, 69
shows at, 68
DisneyQuest, 99–102, xiv
Disney's Old Key West, 18
Disney's Wide World of Sports,
104
getting to, 87
Dixie Landings, 18
The Dolphin
boat service from, 18
Disney-MGM Studios, getting
to, 55
Epcot, getting to, 39
Dolphin Interaction Program,
Sea World, 154
Donald Duck shapes, 33
Doug Live!, Disney-MGM Studios, 67
quick guide to, 58–59
Downhill Double Dipper, Blizzard Beach, 92
Downtown Disney
boat rentals at, 102
boat service from, 18
getting to, 87
map of, 96–97
Marketplace, 98
West Side, 98–102
Dr. Doom's Fearfall, Islands of
Adventure
description of, 136
quick guide to, 132–133
Dudley Do-Right's Ripsaw Falls,
Islands of Adventure
description of, 137–138
quick guide to, 132–133
Dueling Dragons, Islands of Adventure
description of, 140–141
quick guide to, 132–133
Dumbo, Magic Kingdom
description of, 34–35
quick guide to, 24–25

Dynamite Nights Spectacular,
    Universal Studios, 125

E

E. T. Adventure, Universal Stu-
    dios
  description of, 119–120
  quick guide to, 114–115
Early arrivals, 14
Earthquake, Universal Studios
  description of, 119
  quick guide to, 114–115
Easter holiday, 3
The Eighth Voyage of Sindbad,
    Islands of Adventure
  description of, 142
  quick guide to, 132–133
8-TRAX, Pleasure Island, 98
Elway, John, 104
The Enchanted Tiki Birds, Magic
    Kingdom
  description of, 31
  quick guide to, 24–25
Epcot. *See also* World Show-
    case, Epcot; specific at-
    tractions
  behind-the-scenes tours, 13
  boat service from, 18
  don't miss list, 54
  eating in, 52–54
  Future World attractions,
    44–49
  getting to, 39
  map of, 40–41
  monorail routes, 16–17
  night visits, 50
  Park Hopper passes for, 7
  quick guide to, 42–43
  school projects at, 10–11
  shopping at, 54
Ewing, Patrick, 145
ExtraTERRORestrial Alien En-
    counter, Magic Kingdom
  description of, 29
  quick guide to, 24–25

F

Fanny packs, 14
Fantasia Gardens, 103
Fantasmic!, Disney-MGM
    Studios, 68
  off-season times for, 6
Fantasyland, Magic Kingdom,
    34–35
FASTPASS, 15–16, 28
  at Animal Kingdom, 74
  for Rock 'n' Roller Coaster,
    Disney-MGM Studios, 62
  for Test Track, Epcot, 44,
    8
  to Voyage of the Little
    Mermaid, Disney-MGM
    Studios, 66
Fees, parking, 19
Festival of the Lion King, Ani-
    mal Kingdom
  description of, 80–81
  quick guide to, 74–75
Fievel's Playland, Universal
    Studios
  description of, 124
  quick guide to, 114–115
Film for cameras, 14
Fireworks, Magic Kingdom, 36
Five-Day Park Hopper pass, 8
Five-Day Park Hopper Plus pass,
    8
Flextickets
  for Sea World, 147
  for Wet 'n' Wild, 159
Flights of Wonder, Animal King-
    dom, 83
Food. *See also* Restaurants
  at Animal Kingdom, 84
  at Disney-MGM Studios, 69
  in Epcot, 52–54
  in The Land Pavilion, Epcot,
    46
  in Universal Studios, 125
Food Rocks, Epcot, 47
  quick guide to, 42–43

Foreign language projects, 10–11

Fort Wilderness, 18

Four-Day Park Hopper pass, 8

France Pavilion, Epcot, 52

Frontierland, Magic Kingdom, 32–33

Fuji Flyer, Wet 'n' Wild, 158

The Funtastic World of Hanna-Barbera, Universal Studios
description of, 120
quick guide to, 114–115

Future World, Epcot, 44–49

G

Gangplank Falls, Typhoon Lagoon, 94

Garden Grille, Epcot, 53

Gatorland, 157

Geography projects, 10–11

Germany Pavilion, Epcot, 51

Golf, miniature, 103–104

Goofy's Barnstormer, Magic Kingdom
description of, 35
quick guide to, 24–25

Gorilla Falls Exploration Trail, Animal Kingdom, 78
quick guide to, 74–75

Grand Floridian
boat rentals at, 102
boat service from, 18
Epcot, getting to, 39
Magic Kingdom, getting to, 21
monorail routes, 16–17

Grandmother Willow's Grove, Animal Kingdom
description of, 81
quick guide to, 74–75

The Great Movie Ride, Disney-MGM Studios
description of, 64
quick guide to, 58–59

Guest Relations, Walt Disney World, 20

H

The Hall of Presidents, Magic Kingdom
description of, 34
quick guide to, 24–25

Hard Rock Café, CityWalk, 143, 145

Hard Rock Café, Universal Studios, 125

Hard Rock Live auditorium, 145

Hats, 13

The Haunted Mansion, Magic Kingdom
description of, 33–34
quick guide to, 24–25

Hollywood Brown Derby, Disney-MGM Studios, 69

Honey, I Shrunk the Audience, Epcot
description of, 45–46
FASTPASS at, 15
quick guide to, 42–43

The Honey, I Shrunk the Kids Adventure Zone, Disney-MGM Studios, 67
quick guide to, 58–59

The Horror Make-Up Show, Universal Studios
description of, 122
quick guide to, 114–115

Hotels. See also Off-site hotels; specific hotels
Length of Stay pass, 8
monorail route, 16

Hours of operation
early arrivals, 14
telephone number to check on, 3
Web site to check on, 6

Humunga Kowabunga, Typhoon Lagoon, 94

The Hunchback of Notre Dame Stage Show, Disney-MGM Studios
description of, 66–67

The Hunchback of Notre Dame
Stage Show *(continued)*
quick guide to, 58–59
Hunt, Helen, 121

I

If I Ran the Zoo, Islands of Adventure, 132–133
IllumiNations, Epcot, 53
ImageWorks, Epcot
description of, 46
quick guide to, 42–43
Incredible Hulk Coaster, Islands
of Adventure
description of, 136–137
quick guide to, 132–133
The Indiana Jones Epic Stunt
Spectacular, Disney-MGM
Studios
description of, 65
FASTPASS at, 15
quick guide to, 58–59
Indy Speedway, Magic Kingdom,
30
Innoventions, Epcot
description of, 49
quick guide to, 42–43
Island Merchandile, Animal
Kingdom, 84
Islands of Adventure, 108,
127
attractions, description of,
134–143
don't miss list, 144
eating at, 143
map of, 128–129
quick guide to, 132–133
shopping in, 143
Islands of Adventure Trading
Company, 143
Italy Pavilion, Epcot, 51
It's a Small World, Magic
Kingdom
description of, 34
quick guide to, 24–25

It's Tough to Be a Bug, Animal
Kingdom
description of, 75–76
quick guide to, 74–75

J

Jackets, waterproof, 13
January, water parks in, 6
Japan Pavilion, Epcot, 51
Jaws, Universal Studios, 119
description of, 117–118
quick guide to, 114–115
Jimmy Buffet's Margaritaville,
CityWalk, 143, 145
Journey into Your Imagination,
Epcot
description of, 45, 46
quick guide to, 42–43
Journey to Altlantis, Sea World,
148–149
Jungle Cruise, Magic Kingdom
description of, 30–31
FASTPASS at, 15
quick guide to, 24–25
Jurassic Park, Islands of Adven-
ture, 139–140

K

Kali River Rapids, Animal Kingdom, xiv
description of, 82–83
FASTPASS at, 16
quick guide to, 74–75
water canons at, 83
Keelhaul Falls, Typhoon Lagoon, 94
Ketchakiddie Creek, Typhoon
Lagoon, 95
Kilimanjaro Safaris, Animal
Kingdom
description of, 77
FASTPASS at, 16
quick guide to, 74–75
King Henry's Feast dinner show,
161

Kongfrontation, Universal Studios
description of, 121
quick guide to, 114–115
Kraken, Sea World, 148

L

The Land Pavilion, Epcot
description of, 46–47
Food Court in, 46
greenhouse tour, 10
Latin Quarter, CityWalk, 145
Legend of the Lion King, Magic Kingdom, 35
quick guide to, 24–25
LEGO Superstore, Downtown Disney, 98
Length of Stay pass, 8
Liberty Square, Magic Kingdom, 33–34
Liberty Square Riverboat, Magic Kingdom
quick guide to, 24–25
The Little Mermaid, Disney-MGM Studios. See Voyage of the Little Mermaid, Disney-MGM Studios
The Living Seas Pavilion, Epcot
description of, 47
quick guide to, 42–43
school projects from, 10
Living with the Land, Epcot, 42–43
The Lost Continent, Islands of Adventure, 140–142
Lucas, George, 63

M

Mach 5, Wet 'n' Wild, 158
The Mad Tea Party, Magic Kingdom
description of, 35
quick guide to, 24–25
The Magic Behind the Show, Disney Institute, 12

Magic Kingdom. See also specific attractions
Adventureland rides, 30–31
behind-the-scenes tours, 13
boat service from, 18
don't miss list, 37
E-tickets, 9
Fantasyland rides, 34–35
food at, 36
Frontierland rides, 32–33
getting to, 21
Liberty Square attractions, 33–34
The Magic Behind the Show, 12
map of, 22–23
Mickey's Toontown attractions, 34–35
monorail routes, 16–17
off-season times for, 6
parades in, 35–36
Park Hopper passes for, 7
quick guide to, 24–27
shopping in, 36
Tomorrowland rides, 26–30
tunnels under, 12
Maharajah Jungle Trek, Animal Kingdom
description of, 83
quick guide to, 74–75
Main Street Bakery, Magic Kingdom, 36
The Making of ..., Disney-MGM Studios, 67
quick guide to, 58–59
Mama Melrose's, Disney-MGM Studios, 69
The Many Adventures of Winnie the Pooh, Magic Kingdom
description of, 35
FASTPASS at, 15
quick guide to, 24–25
Maps
Animal Kingdom, 72–73
CityWalk, 130-131

Maps (continued)
  Disney-MGM Studios, 56–57
  Downtown Disney, 96–97
  Epcot, 40–41
  Islands of Adventure, 128–129
  Magic Kingdom, 22–23
  Pleasure Island, 96–97
  Universal Orlando, 106–107
  Universal Studios, 112–113
  Walt Disney World, 4–5
  of water parks, 88–89
Marketplace, Downtown Disney, 98
Marvel Super Hero Island, Islands of Adventure, 134–137
Math projects, 11
Mayday Falls, Typhoon Lagoon, 94
Medieval Times dinner show, 160-161
Melt Away Bay, Blizzard Beach, 93
Men in Black, Universal Studios, 108
  description of, 111, 116
  quick guide to, 114–115
Me Ship, The Olive, Islands of Adventure, 132–133
Mexico Pavilion, Epcot, 50
The MGM Backlot Tour, Disney-MGM Studios
  description of, 67
  quick guide to, 58–59
MGM Studios. See Disney-MGM Studios
Mickey Mouse, 33
  in Fantasmic!, Disney-MGM Studios, 68
  meeting Mickey, 35
Mickey's Toontown, Magic Kingdom, 34–35
Mike Fink Keelboats, Magic Kingdom, 34
  quick guide to, 24–25
Mile Long Bar, Magic Kingdom, 36

Miniature golf, 103–104
Monorails, 16–17
  driver's cab, riding in, 17
Morocco Pavilion, Epcot, 51
Motown Café, CityWalk, 141, 143
Mouse Boats, 103
Mousegear, Epcot, 54
Mulberry Street Store, Islands of Adventure, 141
MuppetVision 3-D, Disney-MGM Studios
  description of, 64
  quick guide to, 58–59
Mystery Fun House, 159

N
Nascar Café, CityWalk, 143, 145
NBA City, CityWalk, 145
New Year's holiday, 3
NFL Experience, Disney's Wide World of Sports, 104
The Nickelodeon Tour, Universal Studios
  description of, 124
  quick guide to, 114–115
Norway Pavilion, Epcot, 50
Nye, Bill, 45

O
Off-Kilter, Epcot, 52
  quick guide to, 42–43
Off-season times, 6
  E-tickets, 9
Off-site hotels
  Animal Kingdom, getting to, 71
  buses from, 18
  Magic Kingdom, getting to, 21
One-Day Ticket, 8
One Fish, Two Fish, Red Fish, Blue Fish, Islands of Adventure
  description of, 142
  quick guide to, 132–133
On-season times, 3

P

Pacific Point Preserve, Sea World, 152
Parades
    at Disney-MGM Studios, 68
    in Epcot, 52
    in Magic Kingdom, 35–36
    in Universal Studios, 124–125
Park Hopper ticket options, 7–8
Park hours. See Hours of operation
Parking lots, 19
Paxton, Bill, 121
Peter Pan's Flight, Magic Kingdom
    description of, 34
    quick guide to, 24–25
Pets on Stage, Sea World, 150
Phone calling cards, 13
Photo ops
    at Animal Kingdom, 79
    at Disney-MGM Studios, 66
    at Universal Studios, 121
Pin trading, 54
Pirates Adventure dinner show, 161
Pirates of the Caribbean, Magic Kingdom
    description of, 30, 31
    quick guide to, 26–27
Pleasure Island
    attractions of, 98
    map of, 96–97
Pocahontas Show, Animal Kingdom, 81
Polynesian
    boat rentals at, 102
    boat service from, 18
    Epcot, getting to, 39
    Magic Kingdom, getting to, 21
    monorail routes, 16–17
Popeye and Bluto's Bilge-Rat Barges, Islands of Adventure
    description of, 138–139
    quick guide to, 132–133

Port Orleans, 18
Poseidon's Fury, Islands of Adventure
    description of, 142
    quick guide to, 132–133
The Prime Time Café, Disney-MGM Studios, 69
Priority seating, arranging for, 54
Pteranodon Flyers, Islands of Adventure
    description of, 140
    quick guide to, 132–133

R

Rainforest Café, Animal Kingdom, 84
Restaurants. See also Food
    at Animal Kingdom, 84
    at CityWalk, 145
    at Disney-MGM Studios, 69
    in Epcot, 52–54
    at Magic Kingdom, 36
    in Universal Studios, 125
    in West Side, Downtown Disney, 99
River Adventure, Islands of Adventure
    description of, 139–140
    quick guide to, 132–133
River Country
    attractions, list of, 95
    getting to, 87
River Cruise with Radio Disney, Animal Kingdom, 84
Rock 'n' Roller Coaster, Disney-MGM Studios, xiv
    description of, 61–62
    FASTPASS for, 16, 62
    off-season times for, 6
    quick guide to, 58–59
Runoff Rapids, Blizzard Beach, 92

S

School projects, 10–13
    Camp Sea World, 154

School projects *(continued)*
Disney Institute, 11–13
at Sea World, 153–154
Sealtest Ice Cream Parlor, Magic Kingdom, 36
Sea World, 147–154
educational tours at, 153–154
rides at, 147–149
shows at, 149–150
standing exhibits, 150–152
Serling, Rod, 61
Seuss Landing, Islands of Adventure, 140–141
Seven-Day Park Hopper Plus pass, 7
Seven Seas Lagoon boat rentals, 102
Shark Reef, Typhoon Lagoon, 94
Shoes for touring, 13
Epcot, 42
Shopping
in Animal Kingdom, 84
at Disney-MGM Studios, 69
in Downtown Disney, 98
at Epcot, 54
in Islands of Adventure, 143
in Magic Kingdom, 36
in Universal Studios, 125
Shows
at Disney-MGM Studios, 68
in Epcot, 52
in Magic Kingdom, 35–36
off-site dinner shows, 159–162
at Sea World, 149–150
in Universal Studios, 124–125
Shuttle buses, 18
Six-Day Park Hopper Plus pass, 7
Ski Patrol Training Camp, Blizzard Beach, 93
Sleuth's Mystery Dinner Show, 161–162

Slush Gusher, Blizzard Beach, 92
Smith, Will, 111
Snow Stormers, Blizzard Beach, 93
Snow White's Carousel, Magic Kingdom, 35
Snow White's Scary Adventures, Magic Kingdom, 35
quick guide to, 26–27
Sounds Dangerous, Disney-MGM Studios, 64–65
Space Mountain, Magic Kingdom
description of, 27–28
E-tickets to, 9
FASTPASS for, 16, 28
quick guide to, 26–27
Spaceship Earth, Epcot
description of, 44
quick guide to, 42–43
Spears, Britney, 67
Spielberg, Steven, 118
Splash Mountain, Magic Kingdom
description of, 32
E-tickets to, 9
FASTPASS for, 16
quick guide to, 26–27
Sports
boat rentals, 102–103
Disney's Wide World of Sports, 104
information on, 102
miniature golf, 103–104
Spring break, 3
Star Tours, Disney-MGM Studios
description of, 63
quick guide to, 58–59
Storm Slides, Typhoon Lagoon, 94
Summit Plummet, Blizzard Beach, 90–91
Sunglasses, 13
Sunscreen, 13

The Swan
   boat service from, 18
   Disney-MGM Studios, getting
      to, 55
   Epcot, getting to, 39
Swiss Family Robinson Tree-
      house, Magic Kingdom
   description of, 31
   quick guide to, 26–27

T

Tarzan Rocks at Theater in the
      Wild, Animal Kingdom
   description of, 80
   quick guide to, 74–75
Teamboat Springs, Blizzard
      Beach, 92
Telephone numbers
   Disney Institute, 11, 13
   Disney's Wide World of
      Sports, 104
   Hard Rock Live auditorium,
      143
   phone calling cards, 13
   sports information, 102
Terminator 2: 3D, Universal
      Studios
   description of, 118
   quick guide to, 114–115
Terrors of The Deep, Sea World,
      151
Test Track, Epcot, xiv
   description of, 47–48
   FASTPASS for, 15, 16, 44,
      48
   quick guide to, 42–43
Thanksgiving holiday, 3
Theater in the Wild, Animal
      Kingdom
   description of, 80
   quick guide to, 74–75
Ticket and Transportation
      Center (TTC)
   boat service from, 18
   monorail route, 16

Tickets, 7–8
   for Arabian Nights dinner
      show, 160
   for Capone's dinner show,
      161
   to Disney's Wide World of
      Sports, 104
   E-tickets, off-season, 9
   to Gatorland, 155
   King Henry's Feast dinner
      show, 161
   for Medieval Times dinner
      show, 160
   for Mystery Fun House, 159
   for Pirates Adventure dinner
      show, 161
   to Sea World, 147
   for Sleuth's Mystery Dinner
      Show, 161
   to Universal Orlando, 108
   to Wet 'n' Wild, 158–159
   Wild Bill's Wild West Show,
      160
Tike's Peak, Blizzard Beach, 93
Timberlake, Justin, 67
The Timekeeper, Magic Kingdom
   description of, 29–30
   quick guide to, 26–27
Tinkerbell's Flight, Magic King-
      dom, 36
Tip boards, 14
Toboggan Racers, Blizzard
      Beach, 92–93
Tomorrowland, Magic Kingdom,
      26–30
Tomorrowland Speedway, Magic
      Kingdom, 26–27
Tomorrowland Transit Authority,
      Magic Kingdom, 30
   quick guide to, 26–27
Tom Sawyer's Island, Magic
      Kingdom, 33
   quick guide to, 26–27
Tony's Town Square Café, Magic
      Kingdom, 36

Toon Lagoon, Islands of Adventure, 137–139

Touring tips for Walt Disney World, 13–16

Tower of Terror, Disney-MGM Studios. *See* Twilight Zone Tower of Terror, Disney-MGM Studios

Transportation
boats, 18
buses, 18
car transportation, 19–20
monorails, 16–17

The Tree of Life, Animal Kingdom, 74–75

Triceratops Encounter, Islands of Adventure
description of, 140
quick guide to, 132–133

Tusker House Restaurant, Animal Kingdom, 84

Twilight Zone Tower of Terror, Disney-MGM Studios
description of, 60–61
FASTPASS at, 16
quick guide to, 58–59

Twister, Universal Studios
description of, 121–122
quick guide to, 114–115

Tyler, Steven, 62

Typhoon Lagoon
attractions, list of, 93–95
getting to, 87
surfing lessons at, 93

U

The United Kingdom Pavilion, Epcot, 52

United States Pavilion, Epcot, 51

Universal Orlando. *See also* CityWalk; Islands of Adventure; Universal Studios
getting to, 109
map of, 106–107
tickets to, 108

Universal Studios
don't miss list, 126
eating in, 125
map of, 112–113
parades in, 124–125
photo ops, 121
quick guide to, 114–115
shopping in, 125
shows in, 124–125

Universe of Energy, Epcot
description of, 45
quick guide to, 42–43

Uptown Jewelers, Magic Kingdom, 36

V

Villains in Vogue, Disney-MGM Studios, 69

Virtual Jungle Cruise, Disney-Quest, 99

Voyage of the Little Mermaid, Disney-MGM Studios
description of, 66
FASTPASS for, 15, 66
quick guide to, 58–59

W

Waist pouches, 14

Water bottles, 14

Water parks. *See also* Blizzard Beach; River Country; Typhoon Lagoon
map of, 88–89
selecting a park, 90
tickets to, 93
Toon Lagoon, Islands of Adventure, 137–139

Wayne, John, 64

Web sites, 6
Disney Institute, 11–12, 13
Hard Rock Live auditorium, 145

West Side, Downtown Disney, 98–102

Wet 'n' Wild, 158–159

White Water Rapids, River Country, 95
Wild Arctic, Sea World, 152
Wild Bill's Wild West Show, 160
Wilderness Lodge
   boat rentals at, 102
   boat service from, 18
   Magic Kingdom, getting to, 21
Wildlife Express to Conservation Station, Animal Kingdom
   description of, 79
   quick guide to, 74–75
The Wild West Stunt Show, Universal Studios, 122
Wiley, Jordan, xiv
Williams, Robin, 29, 65
Winnie the Pooh, Magic Kingdom. *See* The Many Adventures of Winnie the Pooh, Magic Kingdom
Winter Summerland, 104

Wonders of Life, Epcot, 48
The Woody Woodpecker Kid Zone, Universal Studios
   description of, 123–124
   quick guide to, 114–115
World of Disney, Downtown Disney, 98
World Showcase, Epcot
   attractions, description of, 50–52
   behind-the-scenes tours, 13
   school projects at, 10–11

Y
Yacht and Beach Club
   boat service from, 18
   Disney-MGM Studios, getting to, 55
   Epcot, getting to, 39
Youngblood, Brennon, xiv
Youngblood, Courtney, xiv

Looking for Love in All the Wrong Places?

Are you stuck in a revolving door of bad dates? Or maybe you've given up on finding a meaningful relationship altogether. According to dating experts David Coleman and Richard Doyle, it doesn't have to be that way. You *can* have that happy, healthy relationship you've been looking for.

With eye-opening exercises, quizzes, and other self-assessment tools, you'll pinpoint specific aspects of your personality that have caused you to pick poorly, remain in bad relationships, or sabotage good ones. Once you understand *why* you choose a certain type of person, you can focus on *how* to choose and attract the right one for you.

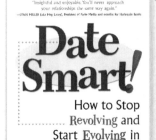

"Insightful and enjoyable. You'll never approach your relationships the same way again."
—LYNN MILLER (aka Meg Lacey), President of Parlo Media and novelist for Harlequin Books

Date Smart!

How to Stop Revolving and Start Evolving in Your Relationships

David D. Coleman "The Dating Doctor"
M. Richard Doyle

ISBN 0-7615-2173-9
Paperback / 288 pages
U.S. $14.95 / Can. $22.00

PRIMA

Available everywhere books are sold.
Visit us online at www.primapublishing.com.